vtiger CRM v5.4.0: User and Administration Manual

Copyright © 2004-2012 crm-now GmbH, Author: Frank Piepiorra

7th Edition

Trade Marks

Many of the designations used by manufacturers and sellers to distinguish their products are claimed as trademarks. Where those designations appear in this book, and crm-now was aware of a trademark claim, the designations have been printed in caps or initial caps. While every precaution has been taken in the preparation of this book, the publisher assumes no responsibility for errors or omissions, or for damages resulting from the use of the information contained herein.

Acknowledgement

The vtiger CRM manual has been in the works since CRM version 4.0.0. Completion of this manual would not have been possible without the help and encouragement of a lot of people. The outstanding vtiger team, its user community, and a number of people contributed technical feedback as this book was being written. I also thank the people who contributed to this manual with informal reviews, suggestions, and fixes during the writing process.

More information about vtiger, the team, the CRM project and its community can be found at:

www.vtiger.com

This manual has been sponsored by the crm-now GmbH. For more Information about crm-now you may look up:

www.crm-now.de

Design: im-netz Neue Medien GmbH

ISBN: 978-1-300-26077-6

Preface

This manual is a comprehensive, step-by-step guide to using vtiger, the powerful Open Source Customer Relationship Management system. The vtiger CRM system is one of the best and most exciting professional-quality Open Source CRM products around, and is intended primarily for B2B companies with longer sales cycles and a stable product or service portfolio.

vtiger provides your organization with an easy-to-use, powerful, comprehensive and integrated solution for managing customer relationships. Because it is Open Source and it provides professional features, the vtiger CRM system has been adopted by a large and growing community.

This manual is based on the official Open Source v5.4.0 release and does not highlight the changes to the previous version v5.3.0. It includes the modules which are released as optional modules.

The manual is intended to be a clear and supportive reference work for vtiger users and administrators. However, this manual is not the official vtiger documentation and does not include documentation intended for in-depth customization and development purposes. I hope to answer most of the questions you might have about the various features and modules of the vtiger CRM. The following subjects are covered in particular:

- General approach of vtiger CRM. With all its modules and their relationship to each other, vtiger CRM can be a bit overwhelming at first. I'll get you up to speed quickly on how the pieces fit together.
- How to start using the CRM system. What should you do first?
- Sales force automation. After you have entered data into the system how the system supports your efforts in an automated fashion.
- Understanding all the relationships. Most data entered into the CRM system is somehow related. These relationships are extensively documented, including their intended purpose. If suitable, examples of proper usage are provided.
- Customizing the CRM system. Each company is different. I explain how you can tailor vtiger CRM to fit your company's needs.
- Security Settings. I explain the principles and the implementation of role-based security.
- Tools. The CRM system comes with a set of tools that supports the organization of sales teams as well as the reporting to management. I show you how these tools can be used.

Table of Contents

1 Introduction 6

    1.1 About this Manual 6

    1.2 Manual Instructions 8

    1.3 First Steps 9

        1.3.1   Becoming a User 9

        1.3.2   PC Setup and other Requirements 9

        1.3.3   Login 10

        1.3.4   CRM Home Page 11

        1.3.5   Access Privileges 16

        1.3.6   How to Start 16

2 *Data Entries for the CRM System* 18

    2.1 Customer Contacts 18

        2.1.1   New Leads 19

        2.1.2   New Organizations 21

        2.1.3   New Contacts 24

        2.1.4   Export and Import of CRM Data 26

            2.1.4.1   Import Contacts 27

            2.1.4.2   Export Data 31

            2.1.4.3   Data Format for Imports 33

            2.1.4.4   Hints for CSV and Excel Formats 34

    2.2 Calendar and Activities 36

        2.2.1   Calendar 36

        2.2.2   All Events and Todos 41

        2.2.3   Import and Export of Activities 41

    2.3 The Sales Process 43

        2.3.1   Leads 43

        2.3.2   Sales Opportunities 47

        2.3.3   Quotes 51

        2.3.4   Sales Orders 58

        2.3.5   Purchase Order 59

        2.3.6   Invoices 62

    2.4 Marketing 64

    2.5 Product - Related Entries 67

	2.5.1	Products	67
	2.5.2	Product Bundles	70
	2.5.3	Price Books	71
	2.5.4	Vendors	72
	2.5.5	Product Import and Export	73
2.6		**Service-Related Entries**	73
	2.6.1	Services	74
	2.6.2	Services Contracts	76
2.7		**Asset Management**	77
2.8		**Project Management**	78
	2.8.1	Projects	78
	2.8.2	Project	79
	2.8.3	Project Tasks	80

3 *Working with the CRM System* 81

3.1 **General Remarks** 81

3.1.1	Working with Lists	81
3.1.2	Tag Cloud	88
3.1.3	Calendar Reminder Popup	90
3.1.4	Chat Functions	90
3.1.5	Tools Menu	90
3.1.6	Send and Receive Emails	93
3.1.6.1	Send Emails	93
3.1.6.2	Send Email Mass Mailing	94
3.1.6.3	Receiving Emails	96

3.2 **Working with the sales process** 102

3.2.1	Working with Leads	103
3.2.2	Working with Opportunities	104
3.2.3	Working with Support	108
3.2.4	Reporting and Analysis	112
3.2.4.1	Dashboard	112
3.2.4.2	Reports	114
3.2.5	Synchronizing CRM with Office Environment	117

3.3 **CRM User FAQ** 118

4 *Administrative Tasks* 119

4.1 **Role-Based Security Basics** 119

Introduction

- 4.1.1 Introduction to Role-Based Security 119
- 4.1.2 Definition of Terms 120
  - 4.1.2.1 Definition of Profiles 122
  - 4.1.2.2 Definition of Groups 125
- **4.2 CRM Administration** **128**
  - 4.2.1 User Administration 128
    - 4.2.1.1 Users Configuration 130
    - 4.2.1.2 User Roles 134
    - 4.2.1.3 Profiles 136
    - 4.2.1.4 Groups 138
    - 4.2.1.5 Sharing Access 139
    - 4.2.1.6 Fields Access 143
    - 4.2.1.7 Audit Trails 144
    - 4.2.1.8 User Login History 145
  - 4.2.2 Studio 146
    - 4.2.2.1 Module Manager 146
    - 4.2.2.2 Picklist Editor 154
    - 4.2.2.3 Picklist Dependency Setup 155
    - 4.2.2.4 Menu Editor 157
  - 4.2.3 Communication Templates 159
    - 4.2.3.1 Notification Scheduler 159
    - 4.2.3.2 Inventory Notifications 160
    - 4.2.3.3 Email Templates 160
    - 4.2.3.4 Company Details 162
    - 4.2.3.5 Mail Merge 162
  - 4.2.4 Other Settings 164
    - 4.2.4.1 Currencies 164
    - 4.2.4.2 Tax Calculations 164
    - 4.2.4.3 Outgoing Server 165
    - 4.2.4.4 Backup Server 166
    - 4.2.4.5 Announcement 166
    - 4.2.4.6 Assign Module Owners 167
    - 4.2.4.7 Proxy Server 167
    - 4.2.4.8 Default Module View 168
    - 4.2.4.9 Inventory Terms & Conditions 169
    - 4.2.4.10 Customize Record Numbering 169
    - 4.2.4.11 Mail Converter 169
    - 4.2.4.12 Workflows 174
    - 4.2.4.13 Customer Portal 179

		4.2.4.14	Configuration Editor 180

        4.2.4.14   Configuration Editor 180
        4.2.4.15   ModTracker 182
        4.2.4.16   Scheduler 183
        4.2.4.17   Webforms 184

5 *Administrations Examples* *187*

5.1 **Example I** **187**
    5.1.1   Example I: settings with groups 188
    5.1.2   Example I: settings with sharing access 190

5.2 **Example II** **191**
    5.2.1   Example II: Settings primary based on groups 191
    5.2.2   Example II: Settings primary based on roles 193

6 *Administration FAQ* *196*

7 *Appendix Resources* *198*

1 Introduction

This chapter explains how to read this manual and provides an overview of the various considerations and preparation a user should go through before starting to work with the CRM system.

1.1 About this Manual

With the help of this manual you will quickly become familiar with the CRM system. The aim of this manual is to bring together the knowledge about the vtiger CRM functions and features with the sales processes, as they are defined by companies using the CRM system. I will explain how to configure the system to fit your needs and how to use it effectively.

Please keep in mind that this CRM system is a tool for your sales, marketing, and/or service organization. It is especially suited for companies:

- which are in the B2B or B2C business
- which have longer sales cycles
- which do not change the product or service offerings frequently
- which are operating with sales, services or marketing teams located at multiple locations

I believe that most vtiger CRM system users and administrators will benefit by reading this manual from cover to cover. Yet, I also know that if you are involved in CRM today, your hectic schedule may force you to skim through this manual to get the highlights, until you can find a quiet moment to read more thoroughly.

So I have tried to make it easy for you. The document has a progressive structure, starting with the basics and becoming more detailed as you move ahead. In addition, references to other useful resources are provided.

The names for organizations or contacts used in the examples of this manual are imaginary. Any resemblances to existing companies or persons are coincidental.

The use of the vtiger CRM software and its related user documentation is subject to the terms and conditions of the applicable licenses.

The Manual's Audience

This manual has been written for vtiger CRM users and administrators. It does not provide any guidance for developers. I expect most readers will have some familiarity with Customer Relationship Management concepts. Although I provide a description of all features as they are implemented at the release date, this book may not be sufficient as your only vtiger CRM reference. This depends on your needs and experience but also on the progress vtiger CRM makes. For a list of some other good resources, consult the Appendix chapter.

The manual is divided into four parts and appendixes:

Chapter 1: Introduction

Describes how the manual should be read.

Chapter 2: Data Entry for the CRM System

Explains how customer contacts are defined and how to use the CRM system to collect customer information. Shows what type of sales activities the CRM system supports and how these activities are being entered. Provides all the information required to understand the sales process supported by the CRM system. All lists possibilities of entering products and price lists to the system.

Chapter 3: Working with the CRM System

Describes how it all fits together and how the CRM system can be used to coordinate the work of sales, marketing and service staff and to increase the productivity of each individual user. Explains all the automated functions available, how sales processes can be defined and which after sales services are offered.

Chapter 4: Administrative Tasks

Describes in detail, how to manage users and privileges and how to customize templates and the CRM system configuration.

Appendix: Administration Examples

Provides some sample configurations and FAQ's for security setups. Explains in detail, how to assign access privileges based on a hierarchical organization structure.

You may get the latest version of this book from the manual's web site at www.vtiger-hilfe.de.

Request for Comments

Please help me to improve future editions of this book by reporting any errors, inaccuracies, bugs, misleading or confusing statements, and plain old typos that you find. Email your findings and comments to the author at vtigermanual@crm-now.de.

Introduction

1.2 Manual Instructions

You can identify the manual version by its ID number located on the second page of this document.

This manual uses the following terms and syntax when explaining procedures and steps:

Menu references

All CRM related menu references are written in **bold**.

> Sample: as shown in the **Calendar** menu.

Menu-based instructions

Instructions to be entered by the menu are also written **bold** and put in brackets. Multiple instructions are separated by the ">" sign.

> Sample: Please click **[Contacts]** > **[New]**.

All screenshots in this manual are based on the actual software release as provided after an installation.

1.3 First Steps

1.3.1 Becoming a User

Before you can start working with the CRM system you must identify yourself to the CRM system as an authorized user. This is done by a login procedure which requires a Username and a Password. Both are provided to you by your CRM system administrator.

1.3.2 PC Setup and other Requirements

For the simple use of the CRM system you do not need to install any software on your computer system. You operate the CRM system solely by way of your preferred web browser. Please note the following minimum requirements and follow the browser setup instructions.

Hardware requirements:

PC or Thin Client with Browser and minimum screen resolution of 1024 * 768 pixels.

> If you want to have your desktop computer software linked to the CRM system, you may install some extensions on your computer later. For this purpose please refer to the appropriate other manuals listed in the Appendix.

Browsers:

Firefox 10.0 or newer, Microsoft Internet Explorer 8.0 or newer, Safari 3.1 or newer; other browsers have not been certified should work well if they are standards-compliant.

Your browser configuration must meet the following requirements:

Cookies

You must allow cookies.

Java

You must have JavaScript enabled in the security settings of your browser.

Caution: Depending on your Browser type and version, there might be a minor bug within page caching that may affect AJAX client performance in some cases. If your CRM system slows down, it is recommended to empty your browser's cache.

1.3.3 Login

Your CRM system administrator will provide you with a URL to be used as the access address to the CRM system at your browser. You will also need the Username and the Password of your CRM account.

Upon starting the CRM software, the Login screen will appear as shown in Figure 1-1: Login Screen. The user must type a Username and Password into the appropriate fields in order to continue. A user may also choose a different Theme or Language after the Login. Username, Password, Themes and Languages are provided by the system administrator. After entering the Username and Password, press <**Enter**>, or the **Login** Button.

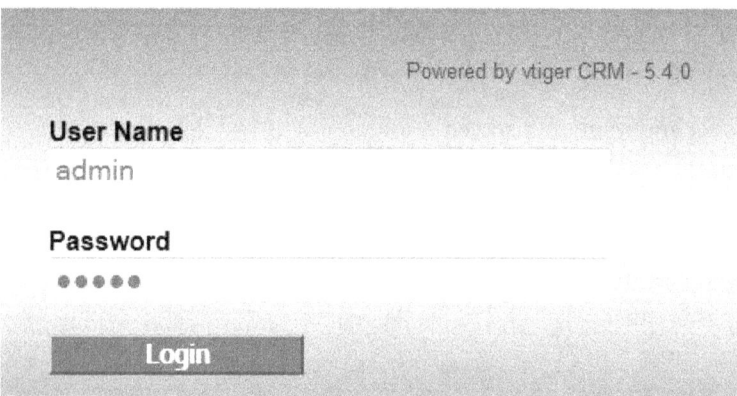

Figure 1-1: Login Screen

Most browsers are able to store your Username and Password to simplify usage. However, this may be a security risk if you cannot make sure that nobody else has access to your computer. Unauthorized persons may get access to your confidential data. This is especially true if you are using a notebook which could be stolen or misplaced.

1.3.4 CRM Home Page

After login, you will see your Home page screen as shown in Figure 1-2: CRM Home Page. Based on the theme you selected, the system settings done by your administrator, and the data stored at the CRM system, your actual screen may look different than the one displayed here. Subsequent chapters will explain how you can customize the Home page and how you can use the CRM functions. Note, that each individual CRM user has his or her own Home page.

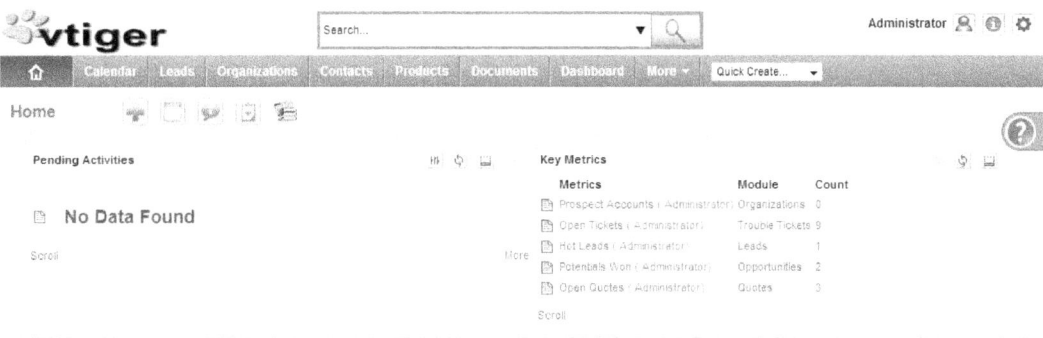

Figure 1-2: CRM Home Page

Home Page Content

The main area of the Home page, as illustrated in the center of Figure 1-2, displays a block summary of the most important CRM information. You may change the order of these blocks by dragging and dropping. You may also change the content of your home page by using the home page edit function or by clicking the appropriate icon at the upper right corner.

Navigation

The smart design of the CRM system will allow you to get most information quickly. You can

> Please note that all data stored in the CRM system has an owner. The owner is marked by an **assigned to:** entry. If you make a new entry, the data will automatically be assigned to you unless you change this intentionally. At the Home page, only data assigned to you will be shown.

navigate within the CRM as if you were browsing a website. It is **not** recommended to use the back and forward buttons of the browser within the CRM. These buttons may cause problems when browsing through pages with dynamically generated content.

It is recommended to use the icons and links provided by the CRM system for navigation. Advanced users may switch to tabbed browsing to speed up the handling process. You may reach each CRM page within a **few clicks. All CRM** pages are in hierarchical order. You may switch between pages at the same hierarchical level or you may access a page directly. **At the Top** of the CRM system as illustrated at Figure 1-3: Screen Top Area, you have access to different area types and functions to navigate and to work with the CRM.

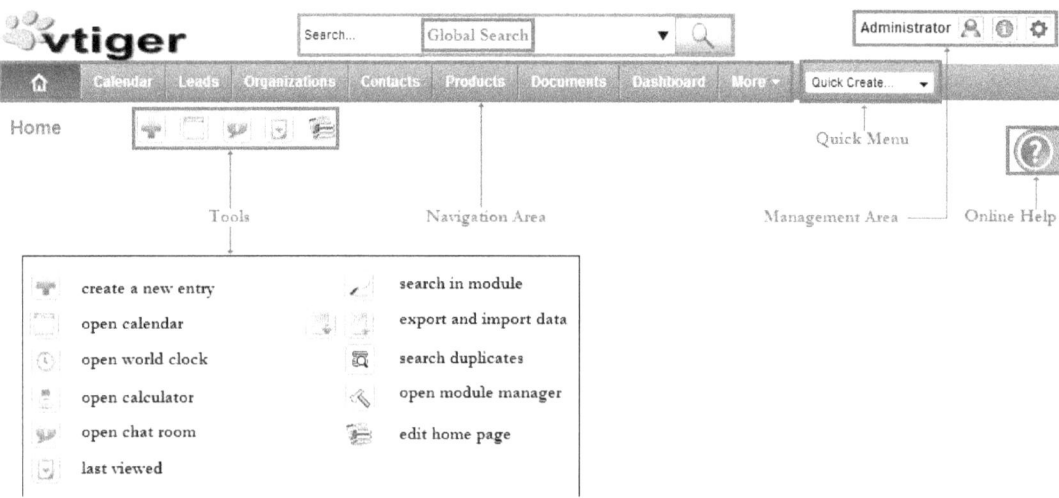

Figure 1-3: Screen Top Area

Table 1-1: CRM Base functions

Navigation area	Function
Management area:	In this area you may access your preference data, get help or release information, or leave the CRM system. The CRM administrator may access from here the Settings menu for CRM configuration.
Navigation area:	In the Navigation Area you may swap between the functions and data lists offered by the CRM system. You may also organize the menu based on your preferences.

Quick Menu:	In the Quick Menu you may quickly reach data entry pages with limited functionality. However, this is a very comfortable entry point for new records if you do not want to leave your current CRM view.
Global Search:	In the Search Area you may search the entire database. You may restrict your search by clicking the icon and selecting certain CRM modules.
Tools:	By clicking these icons, you get a quick access to the calendar, the clock, the calculator and other functions. In addition, you may use the site map menu icon for a quick access to all CRM modules. These icons are only available at the CRM menus when appropriate.
Online Help:	By clicking this icon, a menu with help text related to the current menu opens.

My Preferences

When you click **My Preferences** a new window opens and allows you to view and edit user information and to set your own preferences. Most of these fields are self-explanatory. Some fields which serve special purposes are explained in the following. The **View Audit Trail** button is only functional if the CRM system administrator enables this function. Please refer to Section 4.2.1.7 for further information.

The field marked in Figure 1-4 displays the role assigned to the user. The role provides the users privileges. This field cannot be edited by a user. Only the CRM administrator can be change user's role. Every user can define and change the own password. It is recommended to change the password frequently.

Click the **[Edit]** button to make changes. Alternatively you may move your mouse pointer over an entry. An edit function is then offered, which you can use to change one particular entry.

1. User Login & Role

User Name	admin		Admin	on
Password	Change Password		Email	install@crm-now.de
Status	Active		First Name	
Last Name	Administrator		Default Lead View	Today
Role	CEO		Default Calendar View	This Week

Figure 1-4: Preferences - User Login & Role

More Information:

The field **Signature** marked in Figure 1-5 defines the signature which is automatically added to outgoing emails. You may use HTML tags to format your signature. Note that the space is limited. Your system administrator may increase this space if necessary. At section: CRM Users FAQ you will find more information of how you can format your signature and give it a special look.

Figure 1-5: Preferences - More Information

The field **Internal Mail Composer** defines whether the internal CRM mail composer is used when clicking on an email address. If switched off, the mail composer installed on your computer is used.

> Usernames and passwords have to be a combination of small or capital letters and numbers. It is recommended that you use at least 8 digits. The more digits you have, the more secure CRM access is. The use of special characters such as %, / or characters with accent marks (such as ä, ö, ü or ß), as they are used in some languages, is not allowed. A good password for example looks like Dhe4K39b. User names once created cannot be changed. However, you might create a new user and transfer all data to the new user.

User Advanced Options / Asterisk Configuration:

The fields for the **User Advanced Options** are used to define parameters for communications between your computer (browser) and the CRM server. With the field **Reminder Interval** you define how often your browser will check for pending events. You will see an event as a browser popup when due. The field **Access Key** displays an identification number to be used with CRM extensions and cannot be changed.

```
5. User Advanced Options
            Reminder Interval    1 Minute                        Access Key    ogDyk9SHy7Vr6u9
6. Asterisk Configuration
            Asterisk Extension                                   Use Asterisk  no
```

Figure 1-6: Preferences - User Advanced Option

The fields for the **Asterisk Configuration** are used for a parameter setup of your Asterisk interface. Asterisk is a software implementation of a telephone private branch exchange (PBX) and is used for placing outbound calls by a simple click on a telephone number or displaying information about the caller stored at the CRM if you receive a call by your Asterisk PBX. Before you can use this feature an Asterisk PBX must be installed on your premises.

Home Page Components: The check boxes control the display of content at your CRM's home page. If marked, the content of the selected content will get displayed at Home if data assigned to a logged-in user exists.

My Groups: Each user may be a member of one or more groups. Such a membership is displayed here. Only CRM administrators may change the group membership of a particular user.

Login History: Login history is displayed here, including when you logged in or logged out, and from what computer (by IP address). For security reasons it is recommended to log out every time you leave the CRM system.

Global Search Function

The Home page provides a powerful search function that allows you to search the **entire** database. You may search for any terms. Fill in the search field and hit the icon.

Quick-Menu

The Quick-Menu at Home allows you to jump quickly to an entry page. At the drop down menu select the new entry you want to make. Note that the CRM Administrator may select at the **Module Manager's Layout Editor** the content of this menu.

The Quick-Menu has only limited capabilities for entering data. For the full set of options available look at section Chapter 2: *Data Entry for the CRM System*.

1.3.5 Access Privileges

Your access privileges to the CRM system are set by the administrator when configuring the CRM system. The following privilege types are available:
- The permission to use certain CRM modules.
- The permission to view data in certain CRM modules.
- The permission to edit or to change data in certain CRM modules.
- The permission to delete data in certain CRM modules.
- The permission to export or import data from certain CRM modules.

The CRM system makes sure that you can only exercise certain operations if you have the proper privileges. You may get further information at Chapter *4 Administrative Tasks*. Please contact your system administrator if you want to know more about the privileges set in your system or if you want to have them changed.

1.3.6 How to Start

For optimal utility, the CRM system needs to be configured based on your company's needs. Every user with administrator privileges is allowed to modify the basic settings. All the possibilities are described in Chapter *4.2.1 User Administration* of this manual. In addition, there are many functions available which allow users to configure the presentation of data without changing the basic settings and without administrator access privileges. All the options will be explained in the following sections.

Even without a lot of configuration you will quickly be able to start with the CRM system. Data about customers is the core of each CRM system, so a good way to begin is to start entering data. Since the CRM system is much more than a simple storage system, it is recommended that you make yourself familiar with the sales process as described in Section *2.3 The Sales Process*. Start with entering customer data as a **Lead**. Then convert such a lead into a **Sales Opportunity**. Watch how contacts, organization and opportunities are generated automatically. You may also import lead data from your existing office environment to speed up the process.

As the **first step** it is recommended to start with entering the contact information of your most important active customers. You may add further information later. You will also need to enter your company as an organization and employee's data as contacts. You will need these entries to efficiently communicate with other users. For further instructions please refer to Section *2.1 Customer Contacts*. After you have entered your contacts, you will have a wide variety of automated CRM functions available.

As the **second step** it is recommended that you begin with entering your product and/or service offerings. In Section *2.5 Product - Related Entries* you will find detailed instructions for entering product and service information as well as price books. Again, start with entering only the most important information. You may append the data later.

If multiple users start using the CRM system at the same time, please keep in mind that you have to enter any kind of information only once. Make sure that you communicate with the others.

Use your CRM data immediately when you schedule the next customer contact. Familiarize yourself with the activity functions as they are described in Section *2.2 Calendar and Activities* and define your sales process by different sales stages.

Over time you will improve your capability to operate the system step by step. Within a short time these processes will become second nature.

2 Data Entries for the CRM System

The CRM system offers almost endless possibilities to enter, to process or to display your business data. This includes:

- a **workflow for your entire sales process**, from the first contact with a prospective client to post-sale support, and
- a **contact management** for your customers and vendors, related to individual persons, enterprises or groups,
- a time and priority controlled **activity management,**
- a **product and service catalog.**

You must decide what functions are important to you and your business and what you want to use. The following sections will describe in detail how to enter data into the CRM system and how the data is presented and managed.

2.1 Customer Contacts

The effective administration and utilization of customer contacts is the most important element of a customer relationship management system. Ultimately, all business activities are targeted to customers. The CRM system distinguishes three different contact types:

- Leads
- Contacts to single persons
- Contacts to an organization, such as legal entities, groups, agencies etc.

The CRM enables entering information about each of these contact types and allows linking individuals to organizations, and organizations to one another, as appropriate. While working with the CRM system, contacts will be categorized by their stage in the sales process, such as leads (earliest stage), opportunities (pre-sales stage) or help desk (post-sales stage).

The following example describes a typical sales procedure:

- Contact information for a potential customer before any business has been discussed, and often before any contact has been initiated, is a Lead. At this sales stage it is not clear whether there will be a business opportunity. The Lead contains basic contact information and information about where this contact information came from.
- The Lead status of this contact will be maintained until contact has been established and there is a concrete business opportunity. All activities related to this Lead will be tracked within the CRM.

- Once a business opportunity emerges, the Lead can be converted to an Opportunity. At this time, the data contained within the lead are automatically split out into a contact and an organization and the Lead is deleted. Information about the specific business opportunity is stored as an Opportunity. All the information collected for the Lead is still available but is now split between Contacts, Organizations and Opportunities.

By using this procedure, only those contacts and organizations which represent potential business are tracked separately. To prevent the CRM system from becoming overloaded with useless data, less concrete Leads are segregated and aggregated in a more compact fashion.

It is not necessary to go through the lead conversion process for every contact and organization, however. You may enter new organizations or contacts directly if they do not fit to the described procedure. This might be true for your own employees, existing customers, partners of your company, personal contacts etc.

2.1.1 New Leads

The sales process supported by the CRM has been divided into the following steps:

- Lead
- Opportunity
- Quote
- Sales and Purchase Order
- Invoice
- Service

You will find a more detailed description in Section *2.3 The Sales Process*.

Leads are the initial contact data you have collected for a prospective customer. You might collect leads from your marketing activities such as trade shows, advertisement, presentations etc. It is likely that most of your leads will not lead to a business relationship.

If you want to collect more detailed lead information, you may click the **[Leads]** menu at the navigation area. Use the icon to create a new lead as shown in Figure 2 1. Now you can enter any lead information you have. Click **[Save]** to transfer your entries to the CRM system.

Entry field marked by a "*" are mandatory. (For the CRM Administrator it is possible to decide which fields are mandatory)

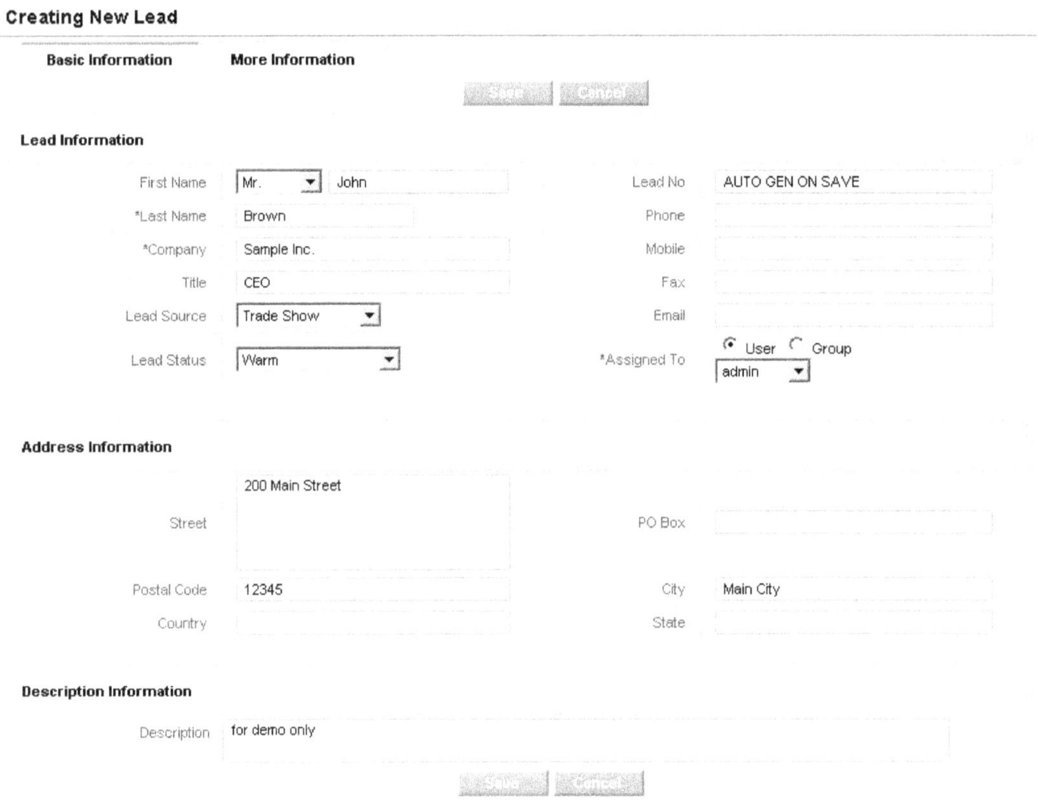

Figure 2-1: New Lead - Basic Information

If you create a lead, it will be assigned to you automatically. You may assign the lead to a different CRM user or user group by changing the content of the "Assigned To" field to a different person or to a team.

2.1.2 New Organizations

The most efficient way to create a new organization from a lead is as described in Section *3.2.2 Working with Opportunities*. However, sometimes it will be necessary to enter new organizations directly. This is helpful, for instance, if you want to have competitors, private contacts or special contacts also stored in your CRM system.

Since organization information can contain references to contacts, it is always advisable to enter the organization information first before you begin entering contact information. When you add a contact to the CRM system later, the related organization information will already be available.

To create a new organization, click **[New Organization]** at the Quick-Create menu as shown in Figure 1-3: Screen Top Area or go to **[Organization]** at the Navigation Area and click the icon. A new window will open as shown in Figure 2-2.

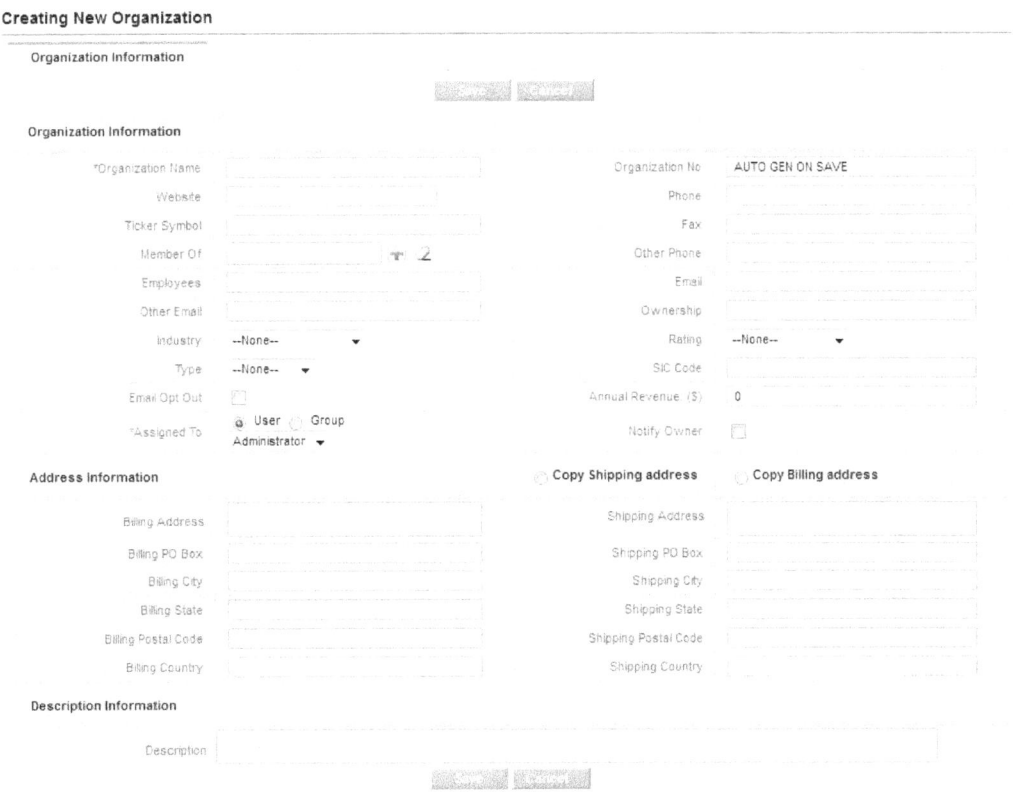

Figure 2-2: New Organization – Master Data

Now you can enter the basic organization information called **master data**. You should only enter information which is relevant to you or to your business. Non-relevant entry fields can remain empty or better should be removed by your CRM system administrator. You may also consider adding customized fields. If several users have write access to the same entry fields, make sure that you agree on a common standard for making entries.

If you want to use the Locate Map function of the CRM system in a country other than the USA, you must add the country information to the address entries.

Click the **[Save]** button to transfer your data to the CRM system.

Like the "Member Of" field some other entry fields refer also to information already stored in the CRM system. These fields are not suitable for direct entries. You have to click the ▼ icon at the end of this line. Then a new window will open that displays the data already stored in the CRM system. When you make a selection this window will close automatically.

Organization Hierarchy

If you have to keep track of a hierarchical order of organizations you may use the "Member Of" entry field as shown in Figure 2-3. This is particularly useful for keeping track of a parent company and its subsidiaries, or companies which are part of a trade organization.

At an organization's detail view click on **Show Organization Hierarchy** to get an overview

Figure 2-3: Call Organization Memberships

about the relationships as illustrated in Figure 2-4.

Organization Hierarchy

Organization Name	Billing City	Website	Phone	Assigned To
Sampe Inc. Headquarters				Administrator
.... **Sample Inc.**				Administrator

Figure 2-4: Display Organization Hierarchy

2.1.3 New Contacts

If you want to enter contact information for individuals, please click **[New Contact]** at the entry Quick-Create menu or go to the **[Contacts]** menu and click the icon. A new window as shown in Figure 2-5 will open.

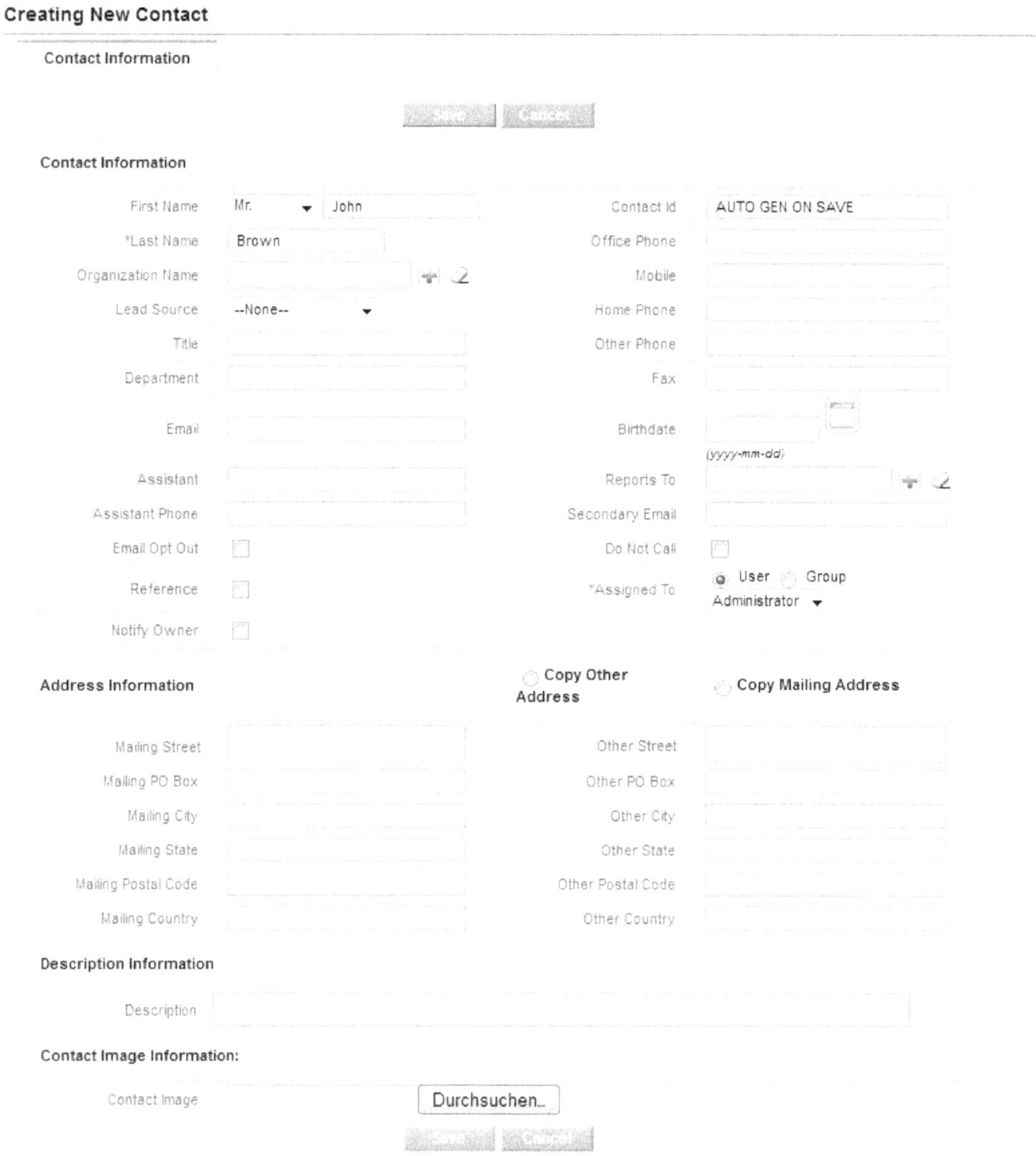

Figure 2-5: New Contact – Master Data

The offered standard fields are self-explanatory.

A Last Name entry should be one word only, if you plan to synchronize your data with Outlook. For instance, if the last name is Mc Murphy make an entry like Mc-Murphy otherwise Murphy will be counted as the middle name.

Make sure that all CRM users agree on the same purpose for each entry field. Your CRM administrator may remove those standard fields which are not suitable for your company based on profiles, or add additional entry fields as explained in Chapter 4.

While most fields are self-explanatory, the following fields serve special purposes:

Table 2-1: Contact Information

Entry Field	Description
Email Opt Out:	Contacts which have this check box selected will not receive email messages such as notifications or ticket information which are normally sent to them by the CRM system automatically. These contacts will also not be available for mass mailing.
Reports To:	Here you may chose the name of the supervisor if the contact has been entered already.
Do Not Call:	Mark this check box to indicate that the contact does not wish to receive calls.
Reference:	You may use this check box to indicate whether this contact is willing to serve as a reference for your business with other customers.
Notify Owner:	When you mark this check box, the CRM owner of the contact will be informed by email automatically whenever another CRM user edits the contact data.
Contact Image:	If available, you may also upload a contact image to the CRM. This image must be in the *.png, *.jpg or *.gif format. Note that this image will be also displayed as an icon at the contacts list view. A mouse over function for this icon is provided at the list view which displays the full image.

If you enable the customer portal for a contact by marking the Portal User check box, the CRM system will automatically generate an email and will sent it to this contact immediately upon your clicking the **[Save]** button. (Your outgoing mail server must be configured.) This email will contain the username and password for accessing the customer portal. It is advised to inform your contact of this automatically generated message in advance by a separate email.

You may also use this entry page also to allow contacts to access the **Customer Portal**. The Customer Portal provides contacts with a limited access to data which are stored at the CRM. Please refer to Section 4.2.4.13 in this manual for further information.

If you do not intend to use the Customer Portal your CRM Administrator may remove the fields from your menu.

2.1.4 Export and Import of CRM Data

The export and import functions will help you to exchange data between your office environment and the CRM system. CRM data can be used by a large variety of other applications at your office.

To export or to import data, click a module name. You will get to a **List View**. At the top of the list, as shown in Figure 2-6, you will find the import and export tools icons. These icons are only active if they have been enabled by the CRM system administrator.

In addition to leads, contacts, organization, and vendors, data for products and opportunities can be imported and exported. Furthermore, documents and emails can be exported. Please refer to the proper sections in this manual for further information.

Figure 2-6: Contact List View Import/Export

The following section describes the import and export function for contacts. If you want to import or export organizations or other modules, you may refer to this description, keeping in mind that some of the specifics will be different. For the import and export of contact data, you may also consider the MS Outlook plug-in for Windows computer or the Thunderbird extension for Linux, Mac and Windows operating systems, as they are provided with the CRM system.

2.1.4.1 Import Contacts

Click the import icon at the Tool tab as shown at Figure 2-6. A new window will open as shown in Figure 2-7. You have to select your data source (CSV file) by browsing your computer or network.

> The CRM system uses a character set internally which is UTF-8 (Unicode compatible) coded. Unicode is an industry standard allowing computers to consistently represent and manipulate text expressed in any of the world's writing systems. Please refer to Annex UTF-8 coding for further information. You may import data which is UTF-8 or ISO-8859-1 coded. If you use data which is based on ISO-8859-1 your data will be converted to the required UTF-8 format automatically.

All of the data you intend to import must contain the mandatory fields as they are marked by a [*] sign at a contacts edit view and values for all your pick lists. You can find sample import data at Section *2.1.4.3 Data Format for Imports*. This section also explains the **Has Header**, **Delimiter** and **Character Encoding Format** parameters and how you can create your own data sources.

Figure 2-7: Contacts Import, Steps 1-3

If your data contain more information as the available fields in the CRM system can provide, you may start to use **User Defined Fields.**

If you have created a file that meets the requirements, you may upload the file into the CRM system by browsing your computer or network (Step 1). Select the format options of your file. (Step 2). If you have only new data to import and have set all references, skip Step 3 and click **[Next]** to continue.

Step 3 provides the option to check for duplicates during an import as shown in Figure 2-8. Duplicates are only recognized if the contents of records have an identical spelling. This is a limitation which always needs to be considered. Therefore, in many cases it is recommended to check for duplicates with other tools before importing.

Figure 2-8: Contacts Import, Step 3

The following table explains the options you have, if a duplicate is identified during an import.

Table 2-2: Duplicate Check During Import

Criteria	Description	Usage
Skip:	If a duplicate is identified, the CRM data remain unchanged and the data set from your file gets ignored.	Use this if you want to import only new data sets.
Overwrite:	If a duplicate is identified, the CRM data is ignored and the data set from your file overwrites the existing data.	Use this if your import data are more accurate as the CRM's data.

Criteria	Description	Usage
Merge:	If a duplicate is identified, empty fields of the CRM data ret overwritten.	Use this if you want to update parts of data sets.

Organization and the Last Name are mandatory fields for Leads. As an exception, you may leave the Last Name field blank in your import data, but you must map this field. If you do not provide a last name, the corresponding lead entry will be filled with '?????'.

If you have to make multiple imports, the CRM offers to store the references you have selected for future use. Mark the check box **[Save as Custom Mapping]** and write a name of this reference into the entry field. Make sure that this name has not been used before. This Custom Mapping will be available at step 4 as **Use Saved Mapping** when you make the next import.

For Step 4, a new window will open as shown in Figure 2-9. At this site you have to link your data with the corresponding CRM fields. You see the header and the first data entry from your file followed by the standard fields as they are offered by the CRM and your custom fields if you have created them beforehand. It is not necessary that you create references for all data types in your file, but you must link the mandatory and all picklist entry fields.

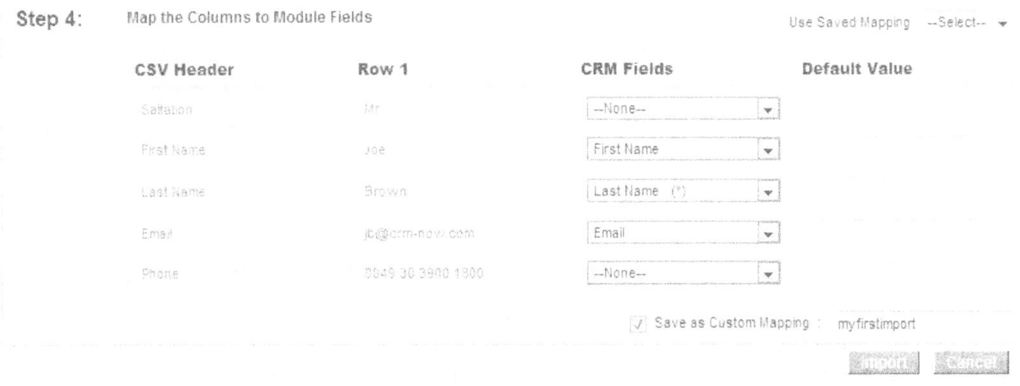

Figure 2-9: Contacts Import, Step 4

At the last import step the CRM shows you the result of the import operation as you can see it in Figure 2-9. Below you will see a list of all imported contacts.

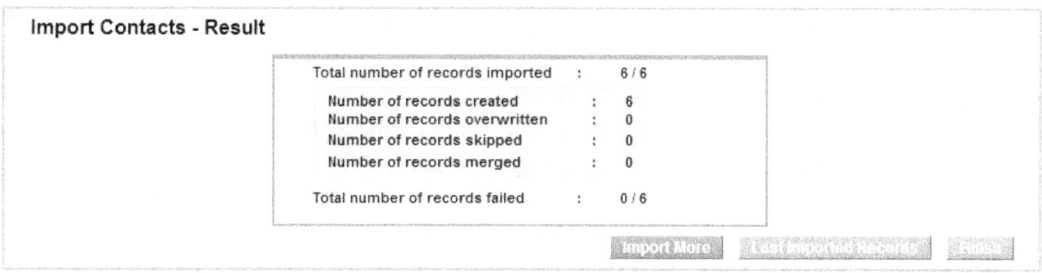

Figure 2-10: Contacts Import, Results

You may review your import data, accept it or reject it.

> If you import contacts with organization information, the import will generate contact and organization entries which refer to each other. During an import the CRM checks whether the contact's organization name already exists. If it does, it will link the imported contact to the existing organization automatically. Therefore, it is always better to import the organization data first.

If you click the **[Last Imported Records]** button a popup window opens which lists the imported data as shown in Figure 2-11. For more details you may open a single data set in a new browser tab.

Figure 2-11: Contacts Import, Data Review

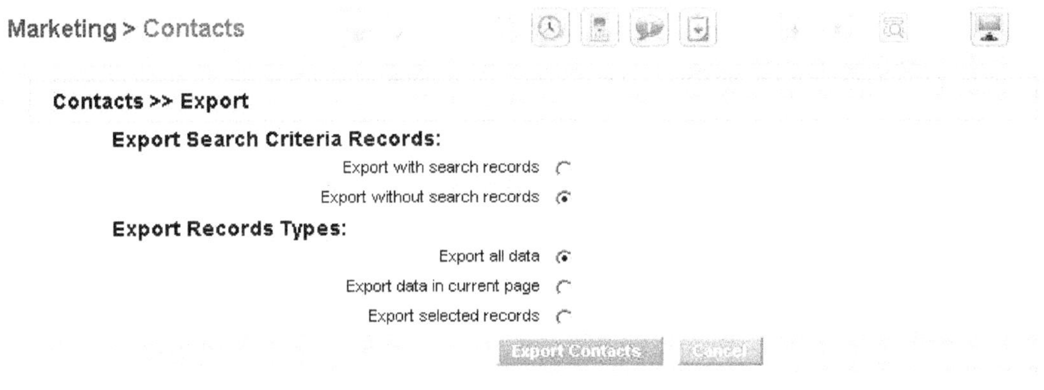

Marketing > Contacts

Contacts >> Export

Export Search Criteria Records:
- Export with search records ○
- Export without search records ●

Export Records Types:
- Export all data ●
- Export data in current page ○
- Export selected records ○

[Export Contacts] [Cancel]

Figure 2-12: Export Selection

If you import a large quantity of data, usually 1000 data sets or more, the import will not get performed immediately but scheduled. Check with your CRM administrator what your data set quantity for a scheduled import is. A scheduled import will get performed automatically and you will get an email when the data are imported.

2.1.4.2 Export Data

You may select the following criteria for your export:

- all records of this module
- only the records you have marked at the list view of this module
- all records which meets your search criteria at the list view of this module
- all data of the current page at the list view of this module without search criteria set

You have to make your decision at the list view about the data you would like to export, before you hit the export icon. For instance, if you would like to export all records of contacts where the last name starts with a **B**, make a search with **B** as your search criteria. Afterwards hit the **export icon** at the list view menu, if this function is available to you, and the menu as shown Figure 2-12 will be displayed.

> Your data is exported in the UTF-8 character format. For further use you may have to convert the data to the character set used at your computer or application. Please refer to the Appendix for further information about UTF-8 and convenient conversion tools.

At this menu you may change you selection criteria if desired and click the **[Export Contacts]** button. A new window for uploading data to your computer opens. The upload window you will see depends on your operating system.

If you click **[OK]**, all data will be exported to your computer. The data is provided as an ASCII file with comma separated values, also called CSV format.

> The format of exported CRM data is different than the data format required for an import. You cannot use exported data for an import directly.

2.1.4.3 Data Format for Imports

Before you can import data you have to format this data in order to meet the CRM's requirements. **The first requirement** is that the data must be presented in the ASCII format with comma separated values (CSV) and UTF-8 or ISO-ISO-8859-1 coded character sets. The CSV file format is often used to exchange data between different database applications. Your file must have the extension csv with lower-case letters.

Since a common standard for the CSV format does not exist, your data sets must be formatted according to the following rules:

- All fields are separated by commas or semicolons and must be individually wrapped by double-quote characters. The separator symbol may get defined by the delimiter parameter during the step 1 imports.
- All data sets must include the mandatory fields (e.g. Last Name and Company for leads).
- All data sets must include values for pick lists (use --None-- if you do not have a value).
- Fields that contain embedded line-breaks or fields with leading or trailing spaces are not allowed.
- Number fields have to contain numbers only without "." or "," characters (for instance, use 3800 instead of 3,800).
- Fields which contain double quote characters should be avoided. If you have to use them, they must be surrounded by double-quotes, and the embedded double-quotes must each be represented by a pair of consecutive double quotes.
- The first record in your file may be a header record containing column (field) names. It is recommended to use a header but if you don't you may remove the header check during the imports step 1. Do not use special characters or Umlaute in the header.
- Dates must be imported in the following format: year-month-day hour: minute: second, for example: "2008-01-07 00:00:00"
- Entries for Multi-Select Combo Boxes must be separated by a |##| character string, for example: "America |##| Europe"
- Check boxes must be imported in the following format: 1 for yes, 0 for no

The second requirement is that you have to include all custom fields with your import if you have created such fields before. In case you do not have any contents for the custom fields, you may leave the field in your data list empty but you must import it. If you do not import these fields, the status of these fields in your CRM's database remains undefined and you can't use such fields for filter functions.

> If your data contains line feed or carriage return characters, you have to remove these before importing the data into Excel. Such characters might be created by the CRM system if you have entries that use multiple lines. This might for instance be the case if you separate street name and suite number in an address entry by an additional line.

```
"Company", "Street", "City", "ZIP", "Country","Phone", "Last name"
"Samples Inc.","123 Samplestreet","Maincity","12345","USA","(123)123-4567","Miller"
"crm-now GmbH", "Main Street 33","Berlin","55555","Germany","","Brown"
```

If you do not have a full set of data available, you must wrap an empty entry by double-quote characters as it can be seen in the sample above for the missing telephone number in line 3. If you have data sets which do not have all mandatory fields included, this data sets will be ignored during an import.

2.1.4.4 Hints for CSV and Excel Formats

The file formats used in Microsoft Excel have become a pseudo standard throughout the industry, even among non-Microsoft platforms. Excel is an application that also produces and uses CSV. Unfortunately, depending on your Excel version the import of CSV data may cause some problems. Some Excel versions do not automatically accept comma separated values. If you experience formatting problems after opening exported CRM data, such as all fields are listed in one column, you may use the following instructions to clean them up:

- Import the CSV file, rather than just opening it. On the Data Menu, choose Import External Data, and then import your data. Browse to the CSV file from the CRM, and click Open. This brings up the Text Import Wizard.
- In step 1, select **Delimited**.
- In step 2, check **Comma**. You will see a preview that shows how the data will be separated.

- In step 3, you can select each column in turn and choose a format. For the CRM date chooses Text and you will get a well sorted Excel sheet.

If you want to import contact data from your office application, you need to make sure that this data is well formed. The following list describes how you may use contact data from your Microsoft Outlook:

1. Check the data format

- Unfortunately, in many cases, data to be imported needs to be checked and modified manually before importing. That is a necessary task to make sure that all data is well formed.
- Export your contact data from Outlook in the Excel format.
- Start Excel and open your data file.
- Look for any special characters such as commas (,) semicolons (;) and double-quotes (") and substitute those, e.g. with a space character.
- Look up the column that contains the mandatory fields. Make sure that each individual data set has a mandatory entry. Do not use any special characters.
- Remove all columns which you do not need at the CRM system.
- Check the content of each individual entry. Make sure that it contains the information you intend to have there. Removing wrong entries later at the CRM system will cause a lot of work. It is better to do it now.

2. Create a CSV file

If you are sure that you have valid and good data, you need to create a CSV file that works with the CRM system. There are tools online available at the vtiger forge (see http://forge.vtiger.com/projects/excelimptool/) which do the formatting for you and exports a well formed CSV file.

2.2 Calendar and Activities

The CRM system provides a calendar such as you would normally find at your desktop. This calendar distinguishes between events and tasks (ToDos), all together called activities. Events are calls and meetings but your CRM administrator may add other types of activities, such as vacation or road show. The operational differences between **Events** and **Tasks** will be explained in the following sections.

> Be careful when scheduling your activities. Even if you consider a meeting as a task, the CRM system does not.

The CRM system offers several possibilities to enter or to schedule calendar-related activities. You might use the calendar directly, the Quick-Menu, or you might create activities during the sales process in Leads or Opportunities, or during services at the Trouble Ticket menu. Calendar entries can and should be linked to other data stored in CRM system, such as contacts, leads or organizations. Not only does the CRM system help you to schedule activities, it also provides you with a set of tools for efficiently managing activities throughout your organization.

2.2.1 Calendar

If you want use the calendar to schedule an event or task, click either on the calendar icon at any list view or **[Calendar]** at the navigation area. A new window will open which will display, depending on your system setup, either the calendars list or the hour view. The hour view is shown in Figure 2-13.

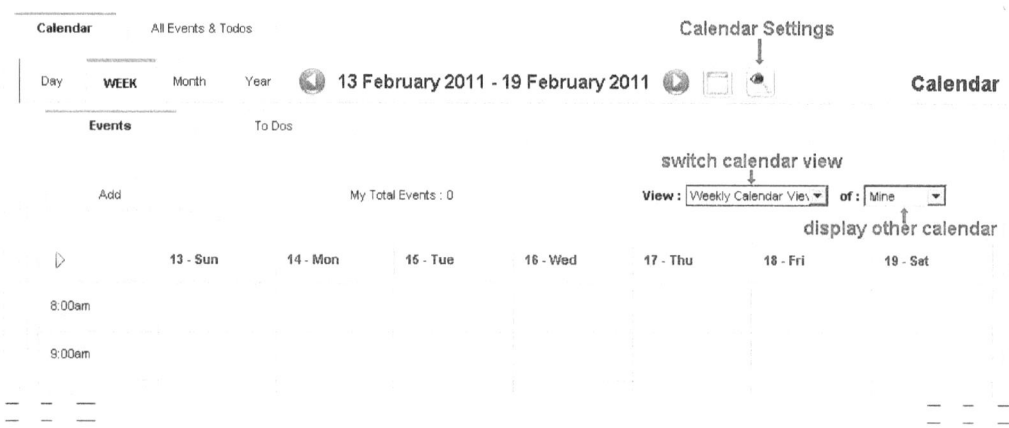

Figure 2-13: Calendar - Hour View

At this view, all events scheduled for a particular day are displayed. You may switch to a weekly, monthly or yearly view by clicking the appropriate icon at the top of the daily calendar. You may also switch to a list view or to the calendar of one of your coworkers. You will get probably the best view on your calendar if you make the weekly view to your standard view.

Adding an Event to the Calendar

To enter the schedule of a meeting, call or one of your own event types click the **[Add Event]** button and select your event type. A pop up window within the calendar will open as shown in Figure 2-14.

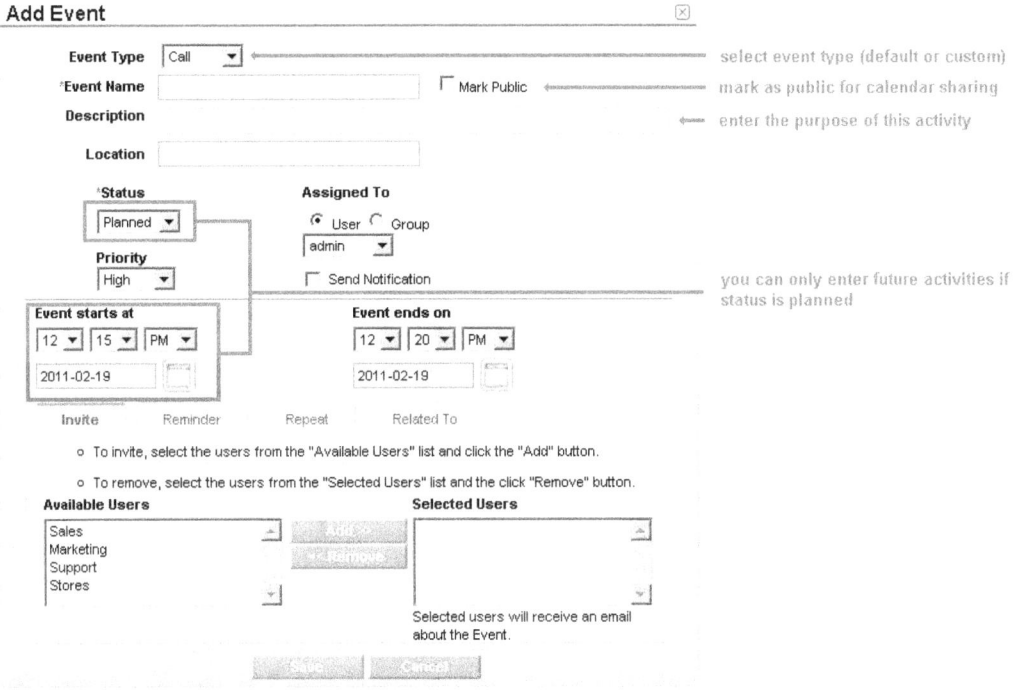

Figure 2-14: Calendar - New Event

Here you may enter your event information. The following table explains the field types.

Table 2-3: Overview event information

Entry Field	Description
Event type:	Select a call or meeting or other custom activities as defined by the CRM administrator.
Event name:	This is a mandatory field and you must provide a name for the activity.

37

Entry Field	Description
Description:	You may add a short description of this event when you plan this event. After the event you may use this space to enter goals, action items, or
Mark Public:	You may mark an event as **Public**, so that a newly created event is shared with other users. Look at section: Calendar Sharing for further information.
Status:	By default the status for a new entry is set to **Planned**. If the status is set to Planned you can only make entries which are dated in the future. If you want to make entries for the past, set the status to **Held** or **Completed**.
Priority:	You may set a priority for an event. Each priority has its own color.
Assigned to:	By default the creating user is the owner of the event. You may change it if necessary.
Send Notification:	If you mark this check box, an email with the actual event information will be sent to the owner of the event. You may use this function for instance if the event owner changes.
Start Date/Time and End:	Every event has a beginning and an end. You may choose to have an end date days later. This is for instance the case if you have business trip of several days.
Invite:	You may invite other CRM users to this event by following the instruction displayed. Note that these users will receive an automatic email with the event information as content

You may click the **[Reminder]** tab, to schedule an automatic reminder email to be sent by the CRM as shown in Figure 2-14.

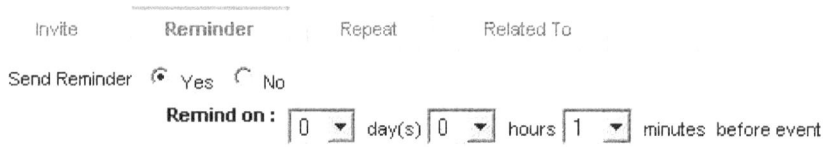

Figure 2-15: Calendar - Event Reminder

For the reminder message you have to enter the time. The current version does not allow you to change the email address. This may change in the future and the mail gets send to the event owner.

In addition, the CRM allows you to schedule events which occur on regular basis. Click the **[Repeat]** tab, to make your settings. The dialog is shown in Figure 2-16.

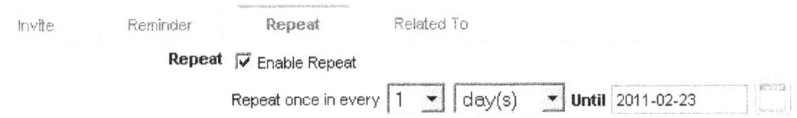

Figure 2-16: Calendar - Repeat Events

Furthermore, you may link an event with your contacts as demonstrated in Figure 2-17.

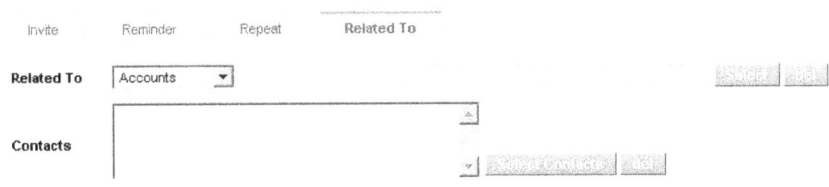

Figure 2-17: Calendar - Event Relations

Finally, click **[Save]** to transfer the event schedule to the CRM. As a result you will see the event listed in your calendar.

A calendar is displayed in the browser defined-language. If you see the calendar in a wrong language, please check your browser settings.

Tasks and To Dos

The CRM system helps you to schedule tasks which are also sometimes called ToDos. Tasks are always assigned to one CRM user or Group and do not have an end date. You cannot invite other users to tasks nor can you link more than one contact with tasks. However, you may transfer tasks to others by changing the owner.

There are many places in the CRM where you can enter tasks. You may enter tasks at any detail view of steps in your sales process or in the calendar. The edit view window as shown in Figure 2-18 will open and you may enter your task information. Please note the mandatory fields.

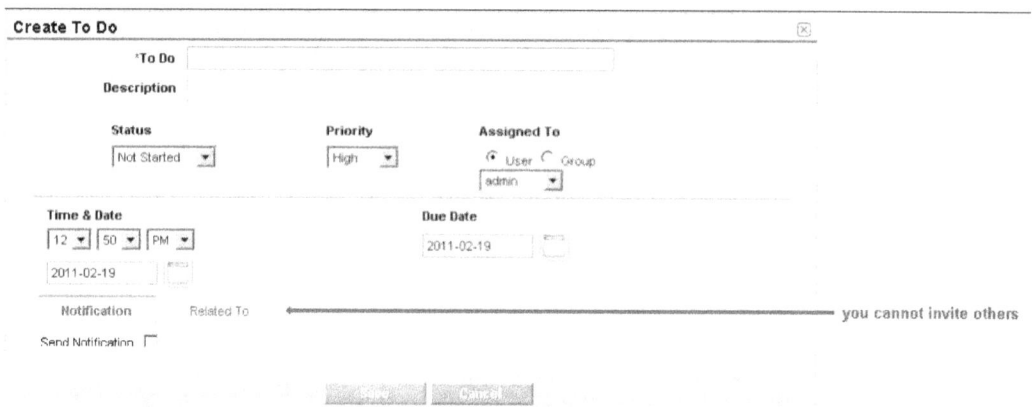

Figure 2-18: Calendar - New Task / ToDo

When you are finished, click **[Save]** to store the task at the CRM system.

Calendar Sharing

By default, every user's calendar is set to private. That means that other users may see that you have an event scheduled but do not get access to detailed information. However, you may share your calendar or specific event entries with other CRM system users by inviting them.

In addition you may setup your calendar settings so that your calendar is shared with other users in the hierarchy as displayed in Figure 2-19: Calendar Settings.

Other users in the role-based hierarchy can also view specific events at another user's calendar if these events have been made public. To make a particular event public, mark the **[Public]** check box as displayed in Figure 2-14: Calendar - New Event when you create a new event. A user with a role above in the hierarchy can always see the calendar of subordinates.

Calendar Settings

You may configure the time your calendar starts and the time format. Please look at Figure 2-19 for further reference

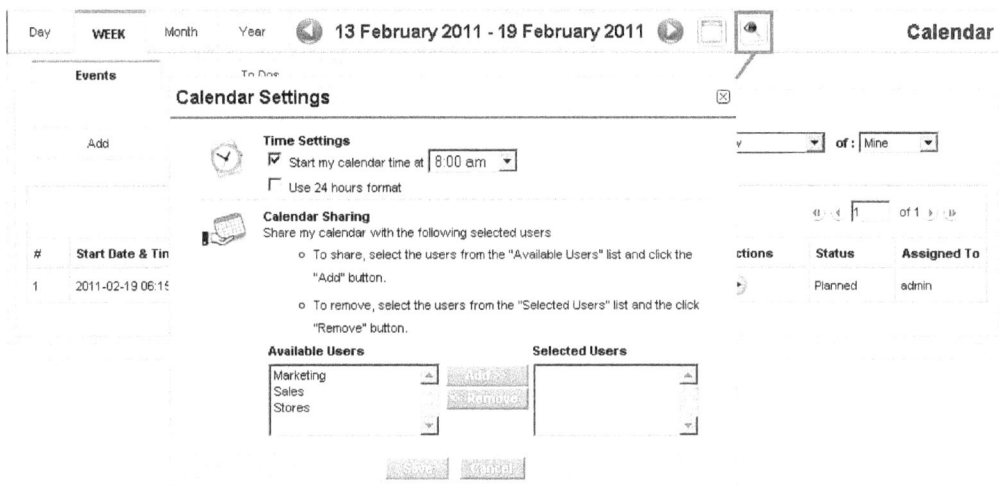

Figure 2-19: Calendar Settings

2.2.2 All Events and Todos

If you want to see all activities in one list you may click the **[All Events & Todos]** tab at the Calendar menu as exemplary shown in Figure 2-20.

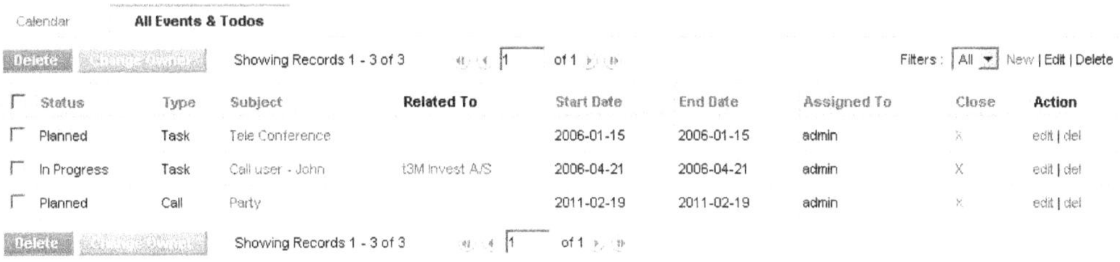

Figure 2-20: Calendar - Hour View

You can change the list according to your own criteria by the filter functions. Please refer to Section *3.1.1 Working with Lists* for further instruction on how to modify the list view. You may also mark an activity as closed by clicking the **[X]** sign.

2.2.3 Import and Export of Activities

For importing or exporting activities to or from your office environment, the CRM comes with a set of extensions to be installed at your computer. This includes an Outlook plug-in for Windows computer or a Thunderbird & Mozilla extension for Windows, Mac or Linux.

For further information on these extensions use the relevant manuals as listed in the manual's Appendix.

2.3 The Sales Process

You may use the CRM system to drive your entire sales process from the first contact with a prospective customer to after-sales services. The CRM system can accommodate the different data and feature requirements at various points in the process. The following sales process phases are offered by the CRM and explained in the following sections:

- Leads
- Opportunities (sorted by different stage, priorities and other criteria)
- Quotes
- Sales and purchase orders
- Invoices
- Help desk with ticket system and FAQ

The sales phases are connected closely with the contact and activity management, product and service catalogues and powerful reports.

Keep in mind that as your contact data progresses from a lead to an opportunity, the CRM system will automatically transfer the requisite data during the progression from one sales phase to another. However, if you find that you need to "jump ahead," going directly to the contact, organization or opportunity phase, the CRM allows this.

2.3.1 Leads

Leads are the first phase in establishing a customer relationship. Your company may get leads from marketing activities such as trade shows, advertisement or PR efforts. At this phase you do not know whether this first contact will lead to a business opportunity. Usually (and unfortunately), most of your Leads will not generate any business. The CRM system considers this by treating Leads differently from all other contact information stored in the CRM. It is sensible to avoid useless Leads burdening the CRM system unnecessarily. For this reason Leads are not linked to other organizations or contacts.

If you create a Lead, you can capture the following customer related data:

- Contact data to a single person or organization
- Description for a lead
- Assessment of value of a particular lead for your company

This data will be stored as master lead data within your CRM. Your administrator may modify the type and amount of master data necessary for your business. As explained in Section *2.1.1 New Leads*, a lead is most likely the best starting point for you to enter customer data into your CRM system. Please refer to this section if you want to create a new lead. Use the Duplicate function as a practical tool if you have to create multiple leads which do not differ much.

If you want to find a lead in your CRM or to add information to an existing lead, go to the **[Leads]** menu at the navigation area. A list of all your existing leads will be shown as illustrated in Figure 2-21.

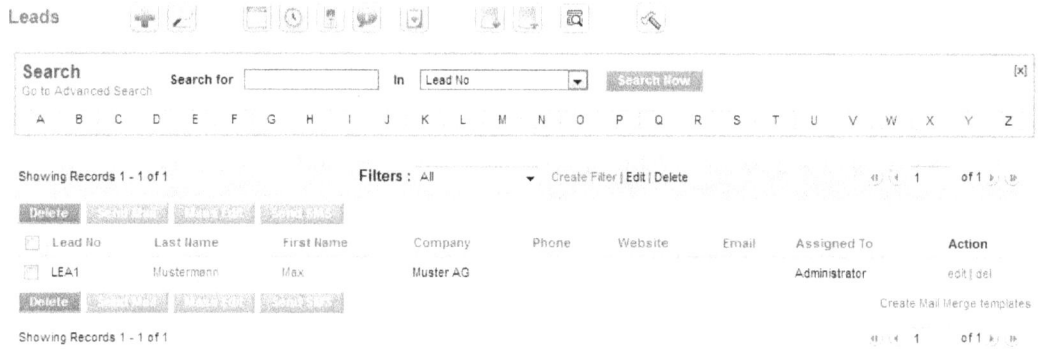

Figure 2-21: Lead - List View

With the search menu, the lead list provides a powerful tool to search and quickly find any particular information as further explained in Section 3.1.1 *Working with Lists - List Search*. At this list view you can also delete leads, or change single or multiple lead entries. Contents of this list can be configured freely to fit your needs. In addition, the CRM can use this list for an automatic analysis.

Lead Details View

In Figure 2-21, some sample leads are already included. To see more information about a particular Lead, click **[Last Name]**. A new window will open as shown in Figure 2-22.

At this site you see the master data of a lead. Once you have provided the full address information, you may want to use the **[Locate Map]** function of the CRM system to see a map of the location. Please note that the default country is the USA. If you want to use the system for a different country, you have to provide the country information with the address information. The CRM links to Google™ Maps for this feature. It will only work, of course, if the target country is covered by the Google™ Maps services.

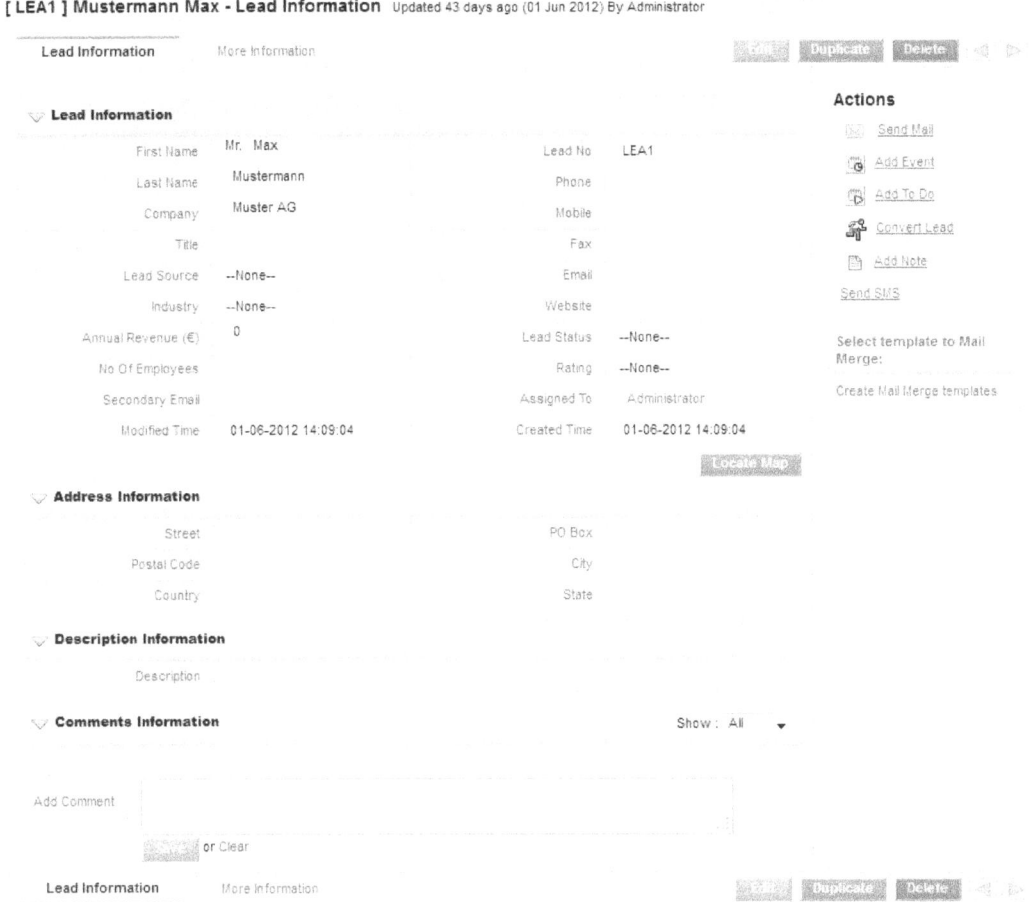

Figure 2-22: Lead Detail View - Master Data

After clicking the **[More Information]** tab you may add further information to this lead as shown in Figure 2-23. Note that the options provided in this menu depend on your CRM configuration.

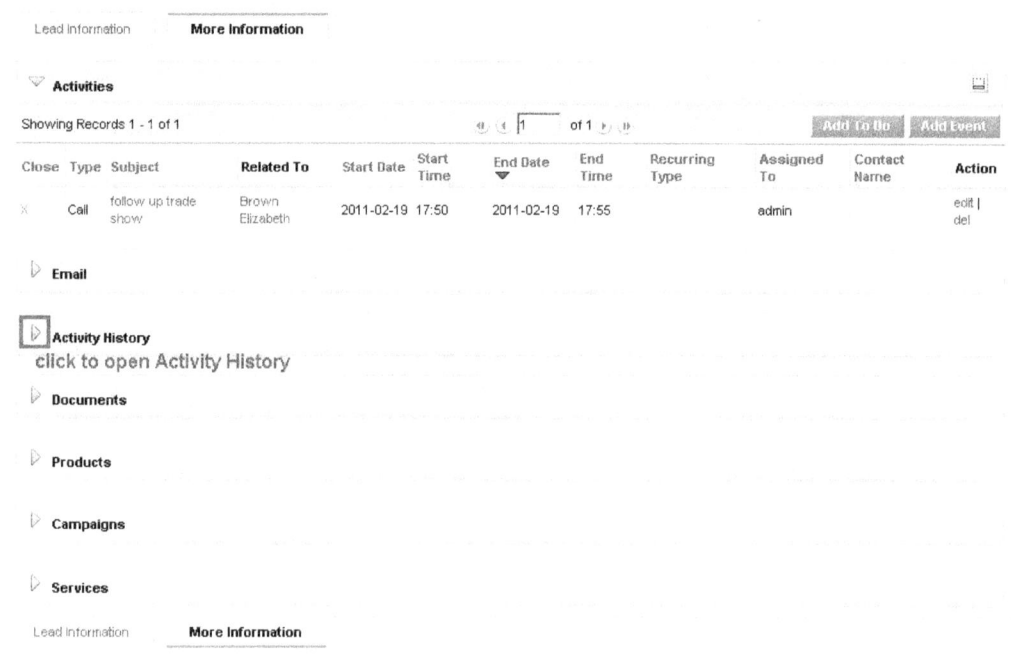

Figure 2-23: Lead Detail View - More Information

Lead Import and Export

You may import or export the list of all leads. To use these functions you will need import or export privileges set by your system administrator. Please refer to Section *2.1.4 Export and Import of CRM Data* for further import instructions. Use the description of the import procedure for contacts accordingly.

2.3.2 Sales Opportunities

In the sales process, sales opportunities are the logical successors to leads. Therefore, you may create a sales opportunity from a lead and transfer all information available for the lead to the new sales opportunity. In addition, you may create a sales opportunity directly. In essence, a sales opportunity is an immediate opportunity to do business with a potential or existing customer. The sales department would expect that an offer could be made for this potential customer in the near future.

Direct Entry of Opportunities

If a sales opportunity arises from a new customer it is recommended that you create an opportunity from a lead as described in section *3.2.2 Working with Opportunities*.

For a new business opportunity with a current or former customer that's already entered into the CRM as a contact or organization, you may enter new sales opportunity directly. Click the ▼ icon at the opportunities' list view. A new window will open as shown Figure 2-24.

Figure 2-24: Opportunity - Create View

Now you may enter your sales opportunity data.

The following table listing refers to the default input mask, which can be changed by your administrator according to your requirements and considers only fields which have special conditions.

Table 2-4: Opportunity Entry Fields

Entry Field	Description
Opportunity Name:	You must give each opportunity a unique name. For a better overview it is recommended to include the organization's name. This field is mandatory.
Amount:	You may set an amount for the expected business. Note that this amount will be used by the CRM to decide automatically whether this opportunity has to be listed at **Home / My Top Open Opportunities**.
Related To:	Select an organization or contact name already stored in your CRM by clicking the ▼ icon at the end of this line. This field is mandatory.
Sales Stage:	Select a sales stage. The stage definition can be configured freely by your system administrator. Every time you make incremental progress in the sales process, you should update this entry.

Be careful in defining sales stages for your company. If you define too many stages, people in

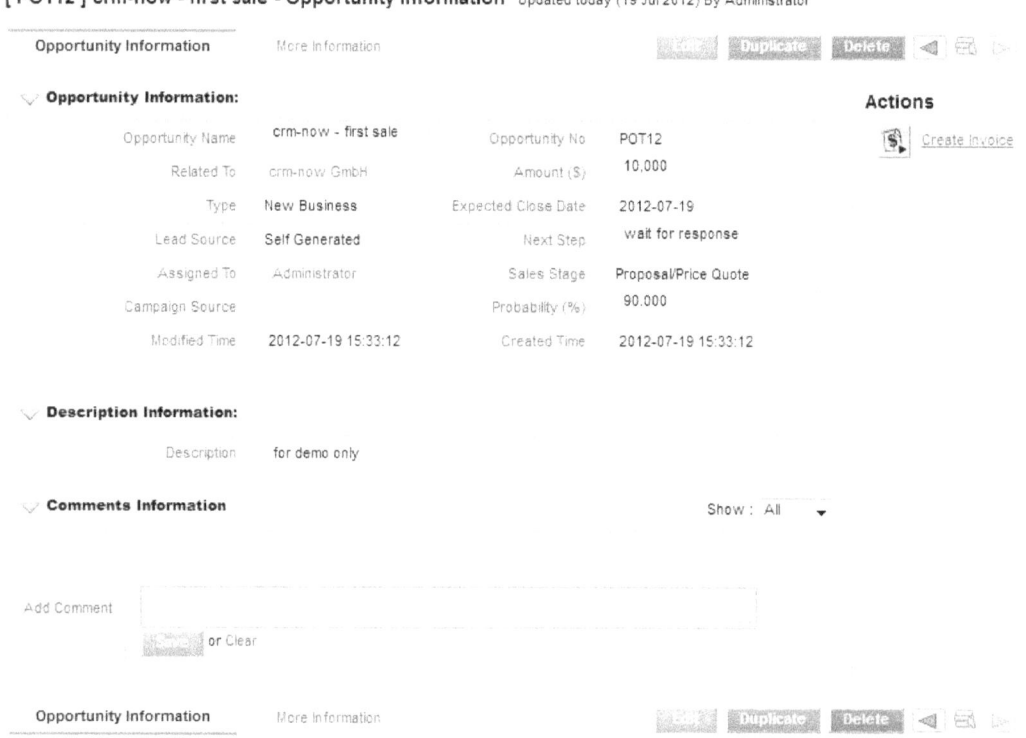

Figure 2-25: Opportunity Detail View - Master Data

your company might find it confusing or daunting to guess which option would be appropriate. Use the extensive possibilities in this input window to store as much information as you have for this opportunity. Come to an agreement with your co-workers on how to use the entry fields.

Additional Information for Opportunities

In order to assign further information directly to a sales opportunity, click the name of an opportunity at the opportunities' list view, as displayed at the **[Opportunities]** menu. You will reach the detail view of the master data as shown in Figure 2-26.

If you click the **[More Information]** tab, you have the possibility of working with the opportunity and to add further information as shown in Figure 2-26.

The related lists which refer to the opportunity are explained in the following table.

Figure 2-26: Opportunity Detail View - More Information

Table 2-5: Opportunities - related lists entries

Reference Type	Description
Contacts:	Here you see a list of contacts related to an opportunity. You may select additional contacts already stored in the CRM
Products:	Here you see a list of products related to an opportunity. You may select additional products already stored in the CRM system.
Sales Stage History:	Every time you change the sales stage, a new entry at this history list will be created.
Documents:	Here you see a list of documents related to an opportunity. You may select additional documents already stored in the CRM system or add new documents.

Reference Type	Description
Quotes:	Your quotes related to this opportunity are listed here. If you create a new quote from here, all master data of an opportunity required for the quote will be transferred automatically.
Sales Order:	All your incoming sales orders related to this opportunity are listed here. You might use the CRM's capability of creating sales orders to keep an overview of your incoming customer orders.

Opportunities Import and Export

The list of sales opportunities can be exported to your computer. You can also load additional sales opportunities from your computer into the CRM system. Check with your system administrator whether you have the permission to execute such operations. The import and export of leads are explained in Section *2.1.4 Export and Import of CRM Data*. You may use the instructions given in this section for the import and export of opportunities accordingly.

2.3.3 Quotes

The CRM system supports you in the creation of quotes for potential customers. You may use one of the following methods:

- You can use the detail view of a sales opportunity to create a quote by clicking at the **[Add Quote]** button at the related list. You may choose this way for an automatic transfer of the opportunities' master data to a quote.
- You may also create a quote directly by clicking at the ⁕ icon at the quote list view. This will require that you have to set all references, for instance to a sales opportunity, manually.

The Figure 2-27 shows the Quote Information and the Address Information blocks for a quote entry.

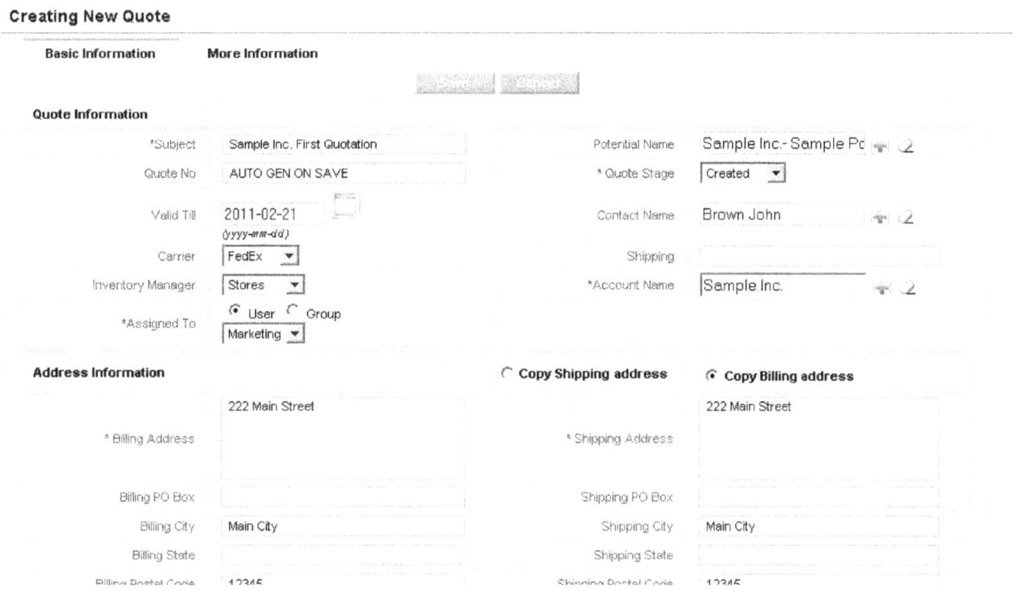

Figure 2-27: Quote - Edit View

A quote relies on your product and/or service catalog and the appropriate price lists, as described in Section *2.5 Product - Related Entries*. Thus, you must have captured your products and services and as well as your prices in the CRM system before you can create a quote.

Quote information

Table 2-6: Special default master data entry fields for quotes

Entry Field	Description
Subject:	You have to give the quote a name. It is practical for a search function to have the customer's name mentioned, e.g. Sample Inc. - 1st Quote.
Quote No:	The quote number is generated by the CRM automatically based on the CRM administrator's setup. Refer to Section *4.2.4 Other Settings - Customize Record Numbering* for more information.
Valid Till:	Enter the expiry date of this quote. This information will become a part of the PDF output.
Team:	This field has been added for your internal use. If you have a team working on this quote, you can note this here.
Inventory Manager:	If you use the CRM to maintain your inventory, you may select the inventory manager here. The inventory manager will receive an automatically-generated email by the CRM system that informs about this quote as soon you hit the **[Save]** button. Your system administrator may change the settings as described in Section *4.2.2.4 Menu Editor*
Organization Name:	You must refer your quote to an existing organization. You select it here by clicking the icon. The CRM will get the address information from this organization and will automatically fill in the corresponding fields at this entry page.

Address information

You must have billing and shipping addresses as part of your quote.

Product Details

For quotes, the CRM system considers all type or discounts which may apply to the offer of products or services. These may include local, state or federal taxes as well as special taxes. These taxes can be calculated individually for each product or service, or calculated for the whole. Before you select products for your quote, you need to decide what tax mode applies to your offer. The CRM system supports an **Individual** and a **Group** tax mode.

The Figure 2-28 displays an example for the entry details for products calculated with the **Individual** tax mode.

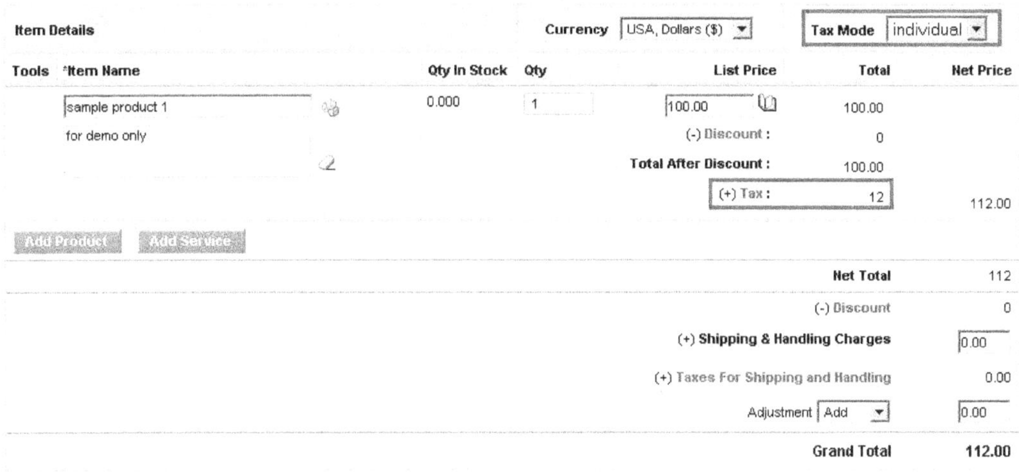

![Figure 2-28 screenshot showing Item Details with Individual tax mode]

Figure 2-28: Quotes - Product Details with Individual Tax Mode

With this tax mode you may set different taxes for each individual product or service you offer.

In Figure 2-29 you see the entry details with the **Group** tax mode. Here the overall tax is calculated after all products or services have been entered. You may add further products or services by clicking the **[Add Product]** or **[Add Services]** button.

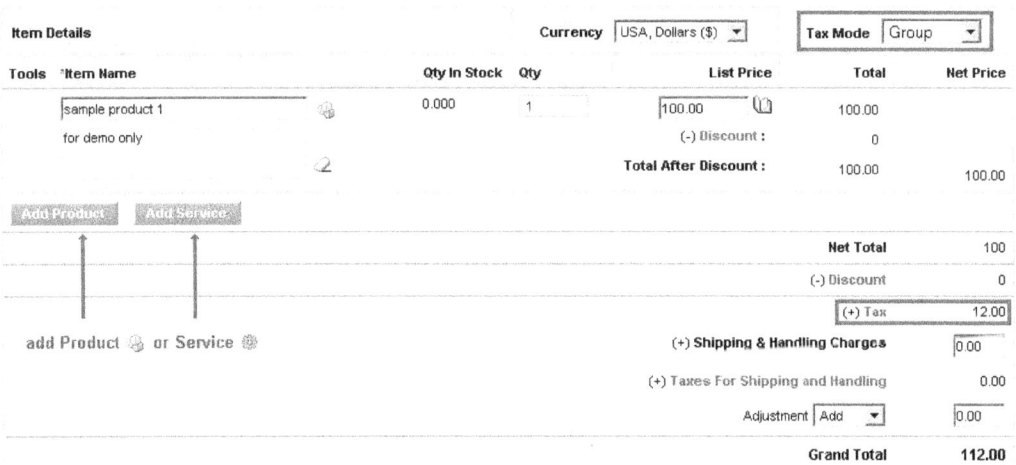

Figure 2-29: Quotes - Product Details with Group Tax Mode

Table 2-7: Quotes - List of default product entry fields

Field Entry	Description
Items:	You must have created a product or service catalog before you can create a quote. Here you have to use the special icons and to select a product or service from the product catalog. You may add an additional comment for each individual product you offer. By default the product or service description is displayed.
Qty In Stock:	After you have picked a product you will see here the quantity in stock. This does not apply to services. Negative numbers could mean that you run out of stock or that no stock has been set up. You may change this number at the products edit view.
Qty:	You have to select a quantity of products or services you offer.
List Price:	Here you enter the customer price. Note that you can use the icon to select the price from your price book entries. That is especially useful if you maintain various price lists for different types of customers.
Discount:	You may select a discount for each individual product or service or a discount for the whole. This discount may be in percent (%) of the list price or may have a fixed value.
Tax:	The CRM calculates your taxes on the basis of the tax information of your product or service catalog. You may modify the calculation for a quote without changing the product catalog entry if required. Taxes which apply to your business are set by the CRM system administrator
Shipping & Handling Charges:	You may add additional shipping charges if applicable.
Taxes For Shipping and Handling:	You may add additional shipping taxes if applicable.
Adjustment:	Finally you can make an adjustment to the quote by adding or deduction a fixed amount.

Product Currency

All price calculations are done in the default currency assigned to a specific user. In addition, the currency assigned to a specific product or service is considered. You may change the currency by selecting a different currency from the list located on top of the product list. If you change a currency the prices for goods or services are being converted to the new currency automatically. The currencies which are available and their conversion rate are defined by the CRM administrator as explained in Section *4.2.4 Other Settings - Currencies*.

Finally the CRM will add up all your entries and will calculate the Sub Total. You may add further taxes or adjustments. Note that the terms and conditions can be defined if you hit the **[More Information]** tab. Your CRM administrator may define default terms and conditions as described in Section *4.2.4 Other Settings - Inventory Terms & Conditions*.

Click **[Save]** to transfer your quote to the CRM.

PDF Output

To provide a PDF copy of your quote, you must have set your company information in advance as described in Section *4.2.2.4 Menu Editor*.

You may configure the Navigation Area of your CRM and create a menu order which fits better to your companies' needs. When you open the **[Menu Editor]** menu, you see at the left side a list of all available and active CRM modules, as illustrated at **Fehler! Verweisquelle konnte nicht gefunden werden.**.

At the right side you see a list of selected module. Be aware of the order. The first 10 entries are displayed at the Navigation Area directly. Beginning with the 11th entry in this list, the menu items are getting displayed at the **More** menu. Menu Editor

You may configure the Navigation Area of your CRM and create a menu order which fits better to your companies' needs. When you open the **[Menu Editor]** menu, you see at the left side a list of all available and active CRM modules, as illustrated at Figure 4-37.

At the right side you see a list of selected module. Be aware of the order. The first 10 entries are displayed at the Navigation Area directly. Beginning with the 11th entry in this list, the menu items are getting displayed at the More **menu.**

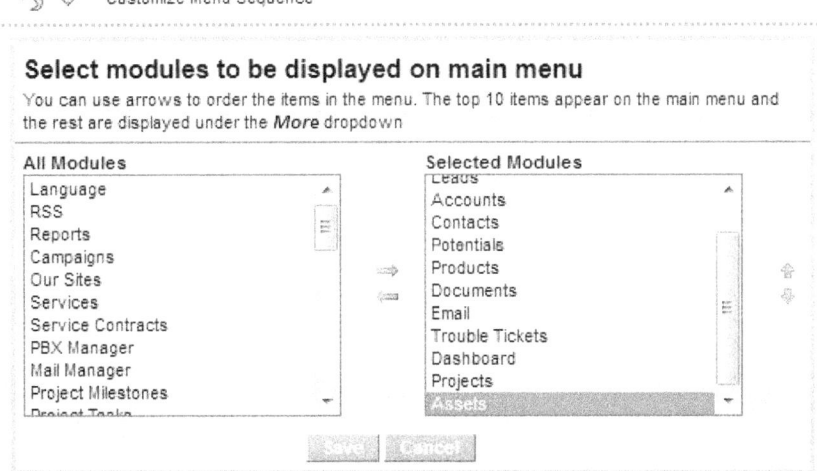

Figure 4-37: Menu Editor - Edit View

You may sort the order on the left side by clicking the blue arrows. You may add or remove a menu by clicking the green arrows. You may not remove the **Home** and the **More** menu. Click **[Save]** to activate your selection.

Communication TemplatesYou may sort the order on the left side by clicking the blue arrows. You may add or remove a menu by clicking the green arrows. You may not remove the **Home** and the **More** menu. Click **[Save]** to activate your selection.

Communication Templates - Company Details. Such a PDF copy can get created and mailed by clicking the appropriate icons at a quote's detail view.

2.3.4 Sales Orders

Sales orders are orders you receive from customers. Such orders of goods or services are usually presented as a paper copy received by fax or mail. It makes sense to capture such orders also in the CRM. A sales order may differ from your quote and you should have such information available at the CRM system.

You may create a sales order from a previous quote by opening the detail view of the corresponding quote and clicking the **[Generate Sales Order]** button. This will automatically transfer your quote information to the new sales order. You may also create a new sales order by clicking the icon at the sales order list view.

In both cases a new window will open as shown in Figure 2-31: Sales Order - edit view for sales order and addresses information.

If you have used a quote before, you will note that all entry fields have been filled automatically.

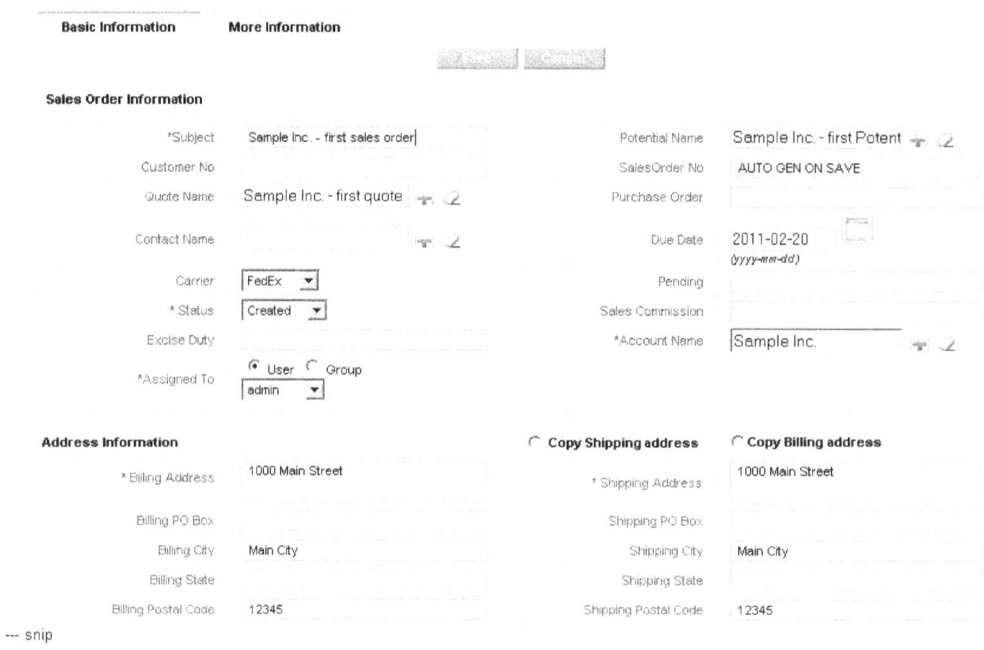

Figure 2-30: Sales Order - edit view for sales order and addresses information

Table 2-8: Sales Orders - Special default master data entry fields

Field Entry	Description
Subject:	You have to give this sales order a name. It is advised to make it unique and to include the organization name.
Sales Order No:	The sales order number is generated by the CRM automatically based on the CRM administrator`s setup. Refer to Section *4.2.4 Other Settings - Customize Record Numbering* for more information.

Address Information

As soon you pick a contact or an organization name, the address information is taken from the contact or organization and included automatically.

Create Recurring Invoices

As illustrated in Figure 2-32: Sales Order - Edit view for recurring invoice information you may add recurring invoice information to a sales order. This means that an invoice will be generated automatically every time the conditions set at this sales order are met.

Figure 2-31: Sales Order - Edit view for recurring invoice information

Product Details

Here the ordered goods and services ordered are listed. Please refer to Product Details in Quotes for more information.

2.3.5 Purchase Order

The CRM supports you also in purchasing goods or services. That might be helpful if you have to order something to fulfill a customer sales order or to maintain your company operation. Before you can enter any purchase orders, you must have the vendor in the vendors list. This is explained in Section *2.5.4 Vendors*. You must have also the products or services to be purchased in your price book.

To enter a new purchase order, click the icon at the **[Purchase Orders]** menu. As another option, you may click the **[Add New Purchase Order]** button at the detail view of a vendor at the **[Inventory] > [Vendors]** menu. By using this option the CRM will transfer the vendor information to the new purchase order automatically.

A new window will open as shown Figure 2-33: Purchase Order - Create View for purchase order and address information blocks.

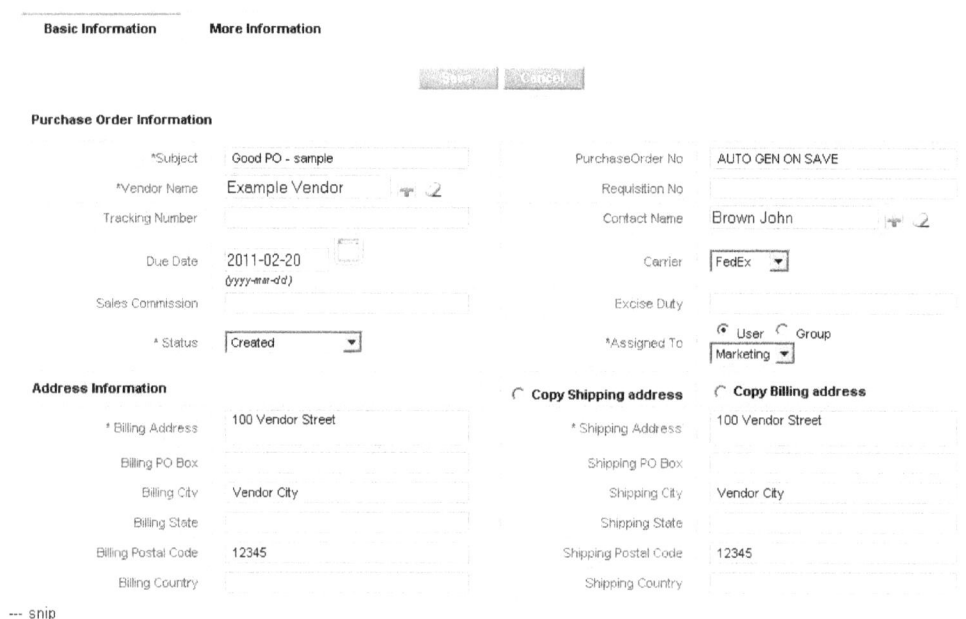

Figure 2-32: Purchase Order - Create View for purchase order and address information blocks

Table 2-9: Purchase Order - Special default master data entry fields

Entry Field	Description
Subject:	You have to give this sales order a name. It is advised to make it unique and to include the organization name.
Vendor Name:	You have to select a vendor name already stored in your CRM system. This will automatically fill in the address information entry fields.
Purchase Order No :	The purchase order number is generated by the CRM automatically based on the CRM administrator`s setup. Refer to Section *4.2.4 Other Settings - Customize Record Numbering* for more information.

The meaning and the function of the other purchase order entry fields are identical to the fields in quotes as described in Section 2.3.3 Quotes.

PDF Output

To provide a PDF copy of your order, you must have set your company information in advance as described in Section 4.2.3.4 *Company Details*. Such a PDF copy can get created and mailed by clicking the appropriate icons at a purchase order's detail view.

2.3.6 Invoices

You may use the CRM system to create customer invoices manually or automatically from a sales order, manually from a quote, or by clicking the + icon at the **[Invoice]** menu. Parts of the detail view of a sample are shown in Figure 2-34.

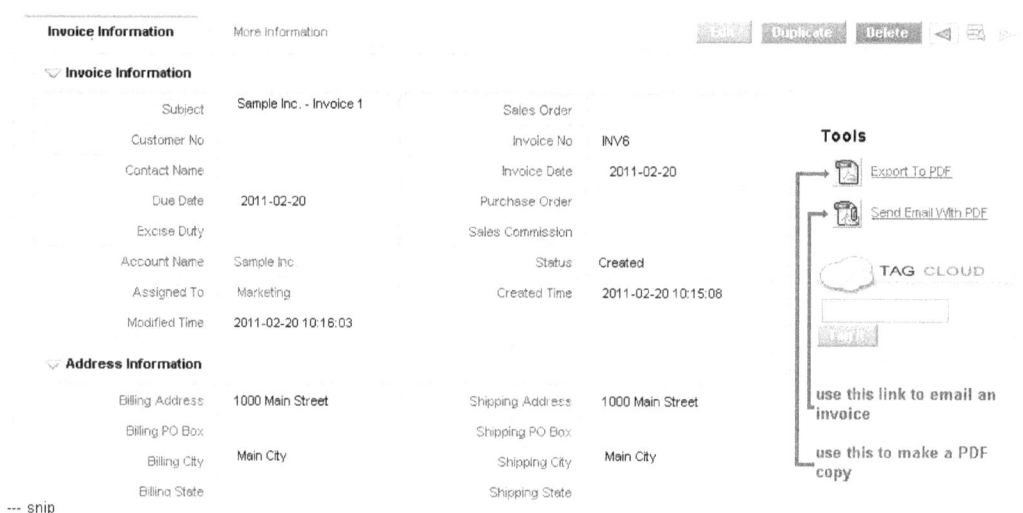

Figure 2-33: Invoice - Detail View

Invoice Information

Table 2-10: Invoice - Special default master data entry fields

Entry Field	Description
Subject:	You must give your invoice a name. It is advised to make the name unique and to include the customer's name.
Invoice No:	The system automatically proposes an invoice number every time you create a new invoice by incrementing from the last existing invoice number. You may define your own standard numbering format for your company as explained in Section *4.2.4 Other Settings - Customize Record Numbering*.
Terms & Conditions :	This information is taken from the CRM administrator settings as explained in Section *4.2.4 Other Settings - Inventory Terms & Conditions*.
Invoice Date:	Every invoice must have a date. You may pick it here.

The meaning and the function of the other invoice entry fields are identical to the fields in quotes as described in Section 2.3.3 *Quotes*.

You may send the PDF copy of invoices as an email to customers directly from the invoice detail view as displayed in the figure. If you click **[Send Email With PDF]** the mail edit window will open which contains the invoice as an attachment allows you to add the recipient and additional text to the email. To create a PDF output you must have set your company information in advance as described in Section *4.2.4 Other Settings - Company Details*.

> You may create recurring invoices from sales orders as explained in Section 2.3.4 *Sales Orders*.

The CRM does not allow you to use an invoice number again. Therefore, in the most cases it is not recommended to delete an invoice once created. Set the amount to 0.00 or better create a credit invoice instead.

2.4 Marketing

The CRM supports your marketing efforts with a **Campaign** module. Click the **[Campaign]** menu to open the list view of your marketing campaigns as shown in Figure 2-34.

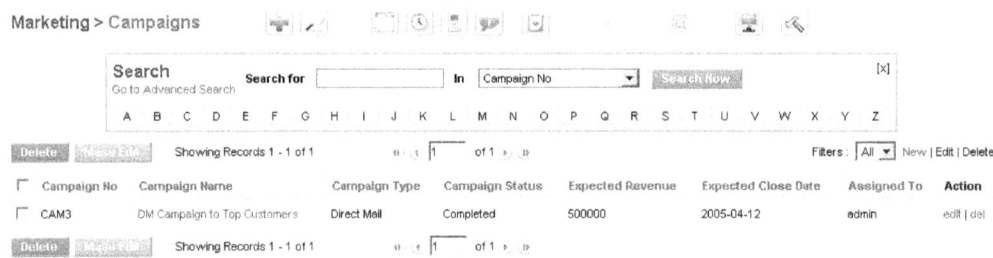

Figure 2-34: Campaigns - List View

You may add a new campaign by clicking the ✱ icon on top of the list. The edit view is shown in Figure 2-36.

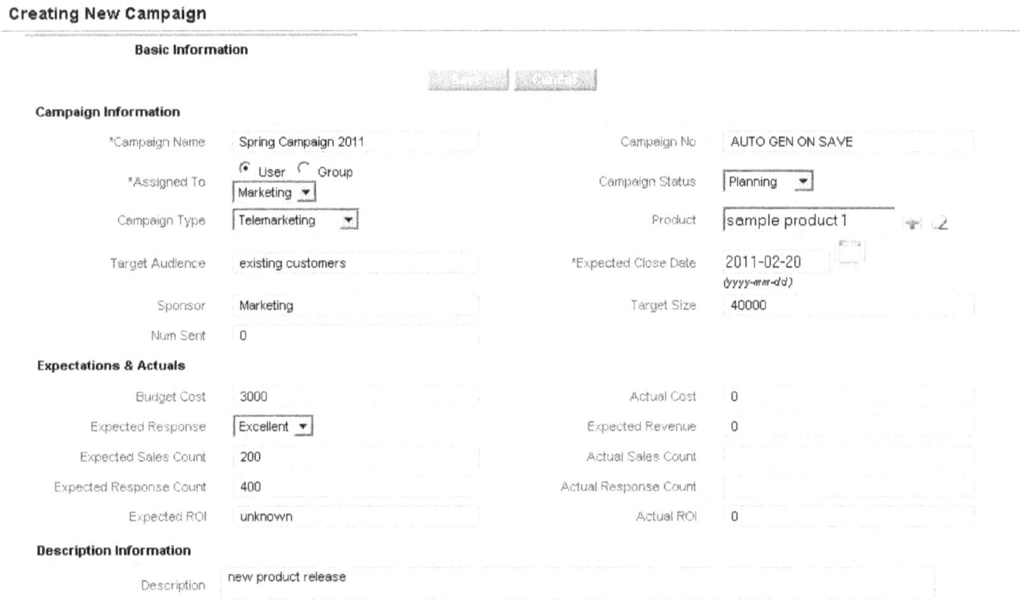

Figure 2-35: Campaign -Edit View

The following table gives you an overview about special entry fields:

Table 2-11: Campaigns - Special default master data entry fields

Entry Field	Description
Campaign Name:	You must give your campaign a short and unique name
Campaign No:	The system automatically proposes a campaign number every time you create a new campaign by incrementing the previous campaign number. You may define your own standard number format for your company as explained in Section *4.2.4 Other Settings - Customize Record Numbering*.

Click **[Save]** to transfer your campaign data to the CRM.

To work with a campaign, open it by clicking the name at the list view. The master data you have had just entered, are displayed.

Click the **[More Information]** tab to add contacts and leads to your campaign as shown in Figure 2-37.

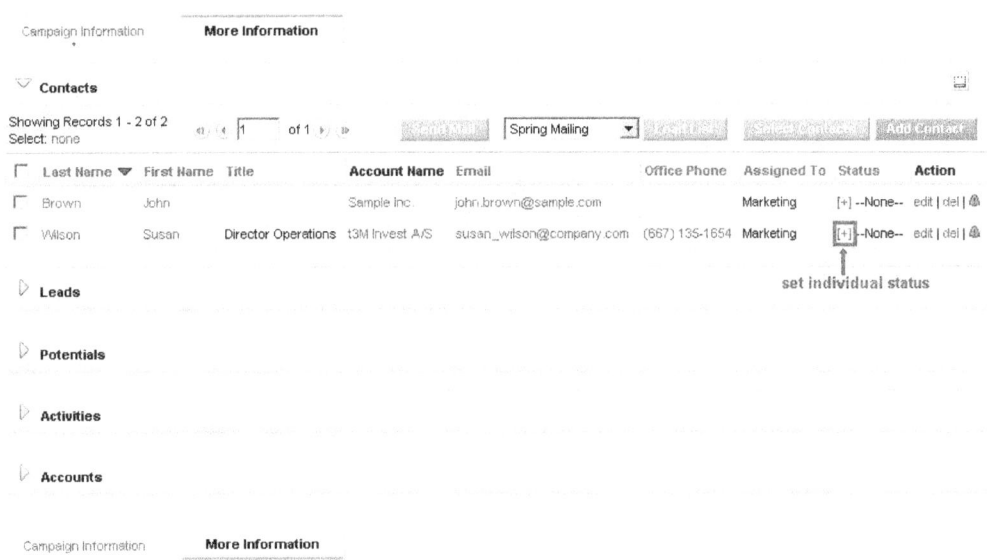

Figure 2-36: Campaign - Detail View - More Information

You may add individual contacts, leads, opportunities or activities to your campaign. Or, you may load existing contact lists or lead lists to your campaign by making the proper selection. These lists must already exist as customized list view in your lead or contact module. Therefore, it is recommended that you create your list views at the Leads and/or Contacts module before you start a campaign. These lists should include the data sets you want to consider in a campaign.

You may send a mass mail with substitute fields to the Leads and Contacts related to a campaign. In Section 4.2.3.3 is explained how you can setup a mailing template with substitute fields which get filled with CRM data automatically. The Status column may be used to track the success of your campaign.

2.5 Product - Related Entries

The CRM uses the term **product** as a comprehensive term for all kinds of goods your company might offer. Similar to a catalog, the CRM provides functions to capture and to categorize your products with various prices and vendors and keeps an inventory if needed. However, for some companies it might be necessary to distinguish clearly between products and services. For this purpose a CRM extension is available as described in Section: Service-Related Entries.

2.5.1 Products

The CRM allows you to link product information with your sales process. To enter a new product, click the icon at the **[Products]** menu for the full set of options. A new window will open as shown in Figure 2-38.

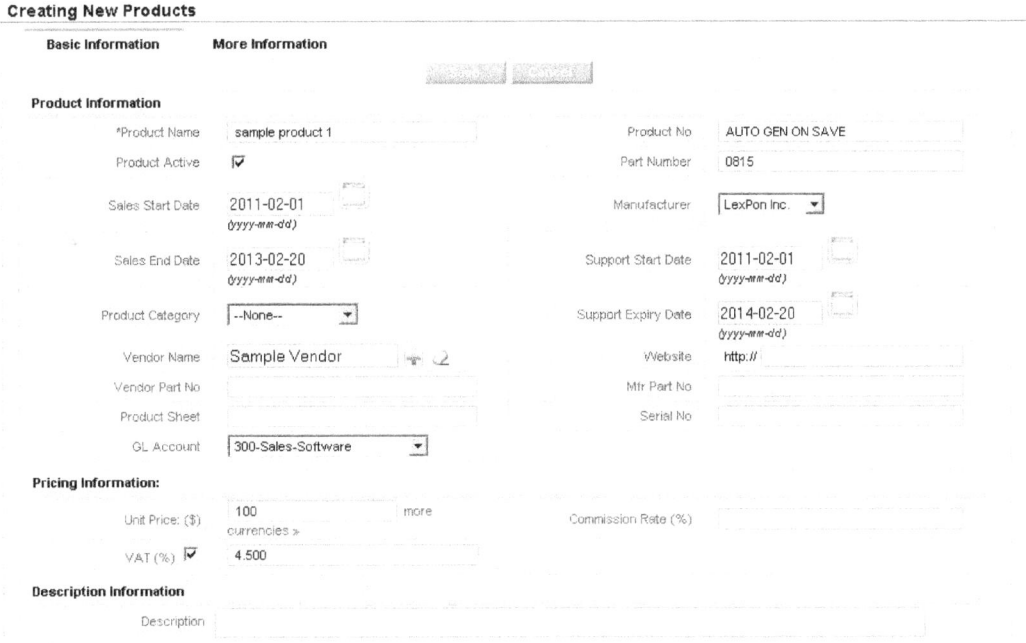

Figure 2-37: Products - Create View - Master Data

The following tables explain the special entry fields for the product's master data.

Product Information

Table 2-12: Products - Special master data entry fields

Entry Field	Description
Product Name:	You have to give each product a name which should be unique.

Entry Field	Description
Product No:	The product number is generated by the CRM automatically based on the CRM administrator's setup. Refer to section: Customize Record Numbering for more information.
Product Code:	You should give each product a unique order code. This could be a combination of letters and numbers. Customers should use this code with their orders.
Active:	By marking this check box, a product becomes active and is available for selection in quotes, orders and invoices.
GL Account:	This entry refers to a General Ledger Account and could be useful if you were importing/exporting items from your accounting program. Each organization in your General Ledge usually has a number for reference.
Description:	This entry will be available at quotes, orders and invoices.

Pricing Information

Table 2-13: Products - Special default master data entry fields for pricing

Entry Field	Description
Unit Price:	You should enter a price per unit. This price may be the list price you pay when you purchase this product from a third party. Note that the selling price can be different as defined in your price lists (see Section *2.5.3 Price Books*). All product prices are entered with the currency as assigned to the user who enters the prices. You have the option to enter a product price in a different currency if the CRM system administrator has configured other currencies.
Tax Class:	You may enter a tax in % that applies to a product. Note that your CRM administrator configures the tax types and rates as explained in section Tax Calculations. Only tax types defined by the administrator will be displayed. You may change the tax amount but not the tax type if necessary.

Stock Information

The CRM supports you in maintaining a stock of goods. You may specify stock information and assign someone responsible for maintaining the stock at the **[More Information]** tab.

Table 2-14: Products - Products - Special default master data entry fields for stock information

Entry Field	Description
Qty in Stock:	You may enter the quantity in stock. This information is used by the CRM when making quotes, orders or invoices. You may use a workflow as described in Section *4.2.4 Other Settings - List Workflows* to control your stock. If you do not intend to use the inventory management features of the CRM system, it is recommended that you set the quantity information to a high number, e.g. 100.000 to avoid low inventory warning messages.
Handler:	You should assign a responsible person for maintaining the stock. This person will automatically be informed by the CRM system if goods are sold.
Reorder Level:	Here you may enter the minimum quantity of goods you want to keep in stock. If the CRM system detects that during the sales process the actual quantity in stock gets close to the minimum amount, the person in charge of the stock will be notified by email.
Qty. in Demand:	Here you may note the quantity of goods you usually buy.

Product Image Information:

You may add up to 6 product images to your product. The image must be in .jpg, .gif or png format and have file extensions with small letters (jpg, gif, png). You should keep the image size as small as possible to avoid time consuming downloads every time you display this CRM page. If you add more than one image, your images will be displayed as rotating cube as shown in the next Figure 2-39:

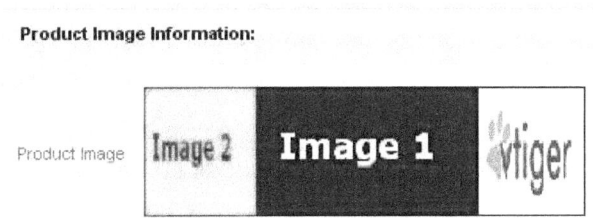

Figure 2-38: Display of multiple images for products

Description Information

Here you have a space for further product information if required. This information will be included into the PDF output of quotes, orders or invoices.

Click **[Save]** to transfer your product information to the CRM system. After saving, the detail view of your product opens. You will see the master data you have just entered. If you click the **[More Information]** tab you have the possibility to enter additional information or to set relations to other CRM modules as displayed in Figure 2-40.

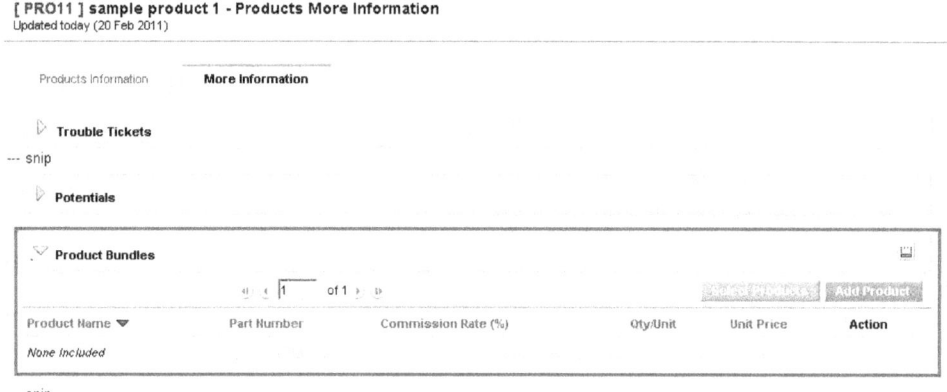

Figure 2-39: Product - Detail View - More Information

Table 2-15: Products - Special related lists entries

Entry Field	Description
Trouble Tickets:	Here you will find all product related tickets. These tickets may be based on customer complains, product bugs, or other customer related after-sales events. You may find further information about tickets at section: Trouble Tickets.
Product Bundles:	Here you may add sub products to your product and bundle these products together for a product selection in quotes, orders or invoices as explained in the next section. Such sub products could be for instance additional parts you are selling in relation to your main product.
Parent Product:	The CRM lists the main product if your product is already part of a product bundle.

2.5.2 Product Bundles

You may create product bundles from your existing product listing but not from services. This feature allows building of a hierarchical products order where you have sub products related to a parent product. A product can be a sub product to an unlimited number of products but a parent product can never become a sub product.

The initial bundle set up is no different to creating a new product or service. Click the **[Add Product]** button shown in Figure 2-40 of a parent product's detail view for the creation of a new related sub product. Enter the product information and save your new product.

To access your product bundles for quotes, orders or invoices, open the product selection menu by clicking on the magnifying glass icon. The new window opens with a list view of your parent products. Click on **[Sub Products]** to see a list of related sub products as illustrated in Figure 2-41.

Figure 2-40: Select Products from Bundle

2.5.3 Price Books

The CRM allows you to work with an unlimited number of different price lists, called price books. This is very helpful, for instance, if your company has different customer types which require a different pricing. You may use special retail, distribution, end customer price lists or others.

Create Price Books

To create a new price book, click the ✱ icon at the **[PriceBooks]** menu. A new window will open as shown in Figure 2-41.

Figure 2-41: New Price Book Create View

You have to give this Price Book a unique name and a currency. You may add a description for future reference. Mark the check box **[Active]** if you want to have this price book available for quotes, orders and invoices. Click **[Save]** to create this new Price Book at your CRM system.

Edit Price Books

To add a product to your Price Books, click the **[More Information]** tab in the Detail View. You may add a product or service to your price book by clicking the **[Select Products]** button. The new window which opens as shown in Figure 2-43, lists all the products stored in the CRM.

You may pick the products you want to add to this price book by selecting the corresponding check box.

You should also set a list price for the product. The entered list price is only valid for this price book. The unit price as set in the product catalogue is shown as a reference. Click **[Add To Price- Book]** to save your selections.

Only activated products are available for selection. If you do not see a product in the selection list, you may check the product status by opening the detail view of this product.

	Product Name	Part Number	Unit Price	List Price
☐	Cd-R CD Recordable	sg-108	313	
☑	sample product 1	0815	100.00	120.00

2.5.4 Vendors

The CRM allows you to enter an unlimited number of vendors which provide goods or

Figure 2-42: Price Books - Product Selection List

services to your company or to your customers. Such vendors are stored separately and not part of the contacts or organizations lists. To enter a new vendor, click the ▼ icon at the **[Vendors]** menu. A new window as shown in Figure 2-44 will open.

After clicking the **[More Information]** tab, you may complete the vendor information by adding contacts, products and other information as illustrated in Figure 2-45. From this view you may also send an email to the vendor.

Basic Information	More Information			
Vendor Information:				
*Vendor Name	My Favored Vendor		Vendor No	AUTO GEN ON SAVE
Category	goods provider			

Figure 2-43: Vendor - Edit View - Master Data

```
[ VEN11 ] My Favored Vendor - Vendor More Information
Updated today (20 Feb 2011)

Vendor Information          More Information
  ▷ .Products
  ▷  Purchase Order
  ▷  Contacts
  ▷  Email
Vendor Information          More Information
```

Figure 2-44: Vendor - More Information

Table 2-16: Vendors - Special default master data entry fields

Entry Field	Description
Vendor Name:	You have to provide a vendor name and should use the vendor corporate name.
GL Account:	This entry refers to a General Ledger Account. In a General Ledger usually each vendor has a special reference number

Click **[Save]** to create a vendor at the CRM system. Your menu will switch to the vendors detail view containing all the information you just entered.

2.5.5 Product Import and Export

By the export and import functions you can exchange data between the CRM and a large number of programs on your computer. All product data can be exported or imported. For starting to import or export, click the **[Products]** menu at the navigation area of your CRM system. The list view of your products will then be shown. Use the icons on top of the list to start the import or export. The icons are only functional if you have the permission to use them. These privileges are set by your CRM system administrator. Please refer to Section *2.1.4 Export and Import of CRM Data* for further export and import instructions. Use the description of the import procedure accordingly for contacts. You can find sample import data in Section *2.1.4.3 Data Format for Imports*. Use the data format described in this section accordingly for your product files.

2.6 Service-Related Entries

You may use **service** for all your company offers which are not related to products. Similar to a catalogue, the CRM provides functions to capture and to categorize your services with various prices and vendors. There is no inventory for services. Services can get combined with product offerings as described in the previous section.

2.6.1 Services

To enter a new service, click the ▼ icon at the **[Services]** menu. A new window will open as shown in Figure 2-46.

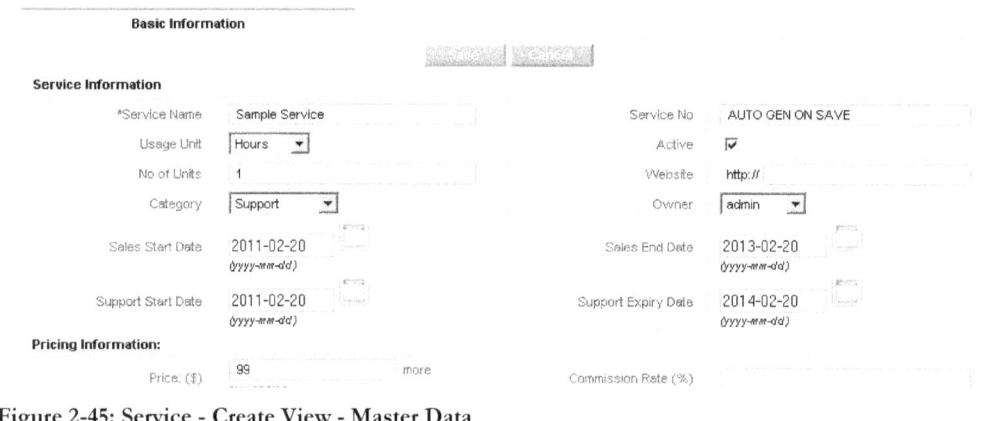

Figure 2-45: Service - Create View - Master Data

Service Information

Table 2-17: Services - Special default master data entry fields

Entry Field	Description
Service Name:	You have to give each service a unique name.
Service No:	The service number is generated by the CRM automatically based on the CRM administrator's setup. Refer to Section *4.2.4 Other Settings - Customize Record Numbering* for more information.
Usage Unit:	Select the usage unit. Note, that the CRM administrator may change the content of the picklist.
Description	This entry will be available at quotes, orders and invoices.

Pricing Information

Table 2-18: Services - Special default master data entry fields for service pricing information

Entry Field	Description

Entry Field	Description
Price:	You should enter a price per unit. All service prices are entered with the currency as assigned to the user who enters the prices. You have the option to enter a service price in a different currency if the CRM system administrator has configured other currencies as described in section: Currencies.
Tax Class:	You may enter a tax in % that applies to a service. Note that your CRM administrator configures the tax types and rates as explained in section. Tax Calculations. Only tax types defined by the administrator will be displayed. You may change the tax amount but not the tax type if necessary

Click **[Save]** to transfer your service information to the CRM system.

After saving, the detail view of your service opens. You will see the master data you have just entered. If you click the **[More Information]** tab you have the possibility to enter additional information or to set relations to other CRM modules.

2.6.2 Services Contracts

To enter a new service, click the icon at the **[Service Contracts]** menu. A new window will open as shown in Figure 2-47.

Figure 2-46: Service Contract- Create View - Master Data

Service Contract Information

Table 2-19: Service Contracts - Special default master data entry fields

Entry Field	Description
Service Name:	You have to give each service a unique name.
Related to:	You should assign the contract either to a contact or to an organization already stored at your CRM.
Tracking Unit:	Select the usage unit. Note that the CRM administrator may change the content of the picklist.
Total Units:	This is the total of the tracking units which are part of the contract.
Used Units:	Here you may enter how many units has been already part of the service you provided. Note that based on this number the percentage value for the contract completion at the Service Contract List view will get computed.

Click **[Save]** to transfer your service contract information to the CRM system. After saving, the detail view of your service opens. You will see the master data you have just entered. If you click the **[More Information]** tab you have the possibility to set relations to trouble tickets, documents or other related information.

2.7 Asset Management

If you deliver goods which require special follow up services, the CRM's asset module provides the necessary tracking functions related to serial numbers or other product attributes. To enter a new asset, click the ⌃ icon at the **[Asset]** menu. A new window will open as shown in Figure 2-48. The offered standard fields are self-explanatory but some have a special purpose.

Creating New Asset

Basic Information

Asset Information

Asset No	AUTO GEN ON SAVE	*Product Name	sample product 1
*Serial Number	1234567	*Assigned To	◉ User ○ Group / Sales
*Date Sold	2011-02-20 (yyyy-mm-dd)	*Date in Service	2011-02-20 (yyyy-mm-dd)
*Status	In Service	Tag Number	
Invoice Name		Shipping Method	
Shipping Tracking Number		*Asset Name	Copy Machines
*Customer Name	EDFG Group Limited		

Notes

Notes	for demo only

Figure 2-47: Asset - Create View - Master Data

Asset Information

Table 2-20: Assets - Special default master data entry fields

Entry Field	Description
Product Name:	You have to provide the related product name. This information is needed to link assets and product information.
Asset No:	The asset number is generated by the CRM automatically based on the CRM administrator's setup. Refer to Section *4.2.4 Other Settings - Customize Record Numbering* for more information.
Serial Number:	Provide the serial number of this product.
Asset Name:	You may use this field for asset classifications.

Click **[Save]** to transfer your asset information to the CRM system. After saving, the detail view of your asset opens. You will see the master data you have just entered. If you click the **[More Information]** tab you have the possibility to set relations to trouble tickets and documents.

2.8 Project Management

This menu is only available if you have installed the appropriate optional CRM package. The CRM may support you in your project management by providing all the information necessary to plan, organize and managing resources for a successful completion of specific project goals and objectives. The CRM's project management is focused on collecting project specific data and it is related to milestones and tasks. It will help you to keep track on a project progress and its related sales process

2.8.1 Projects

To create a new project, click the icon at the **[Projects]** menu. A new window will open as shown in Figure 2-49. The offered standard fields are self-explanatory but some have a special purpose.

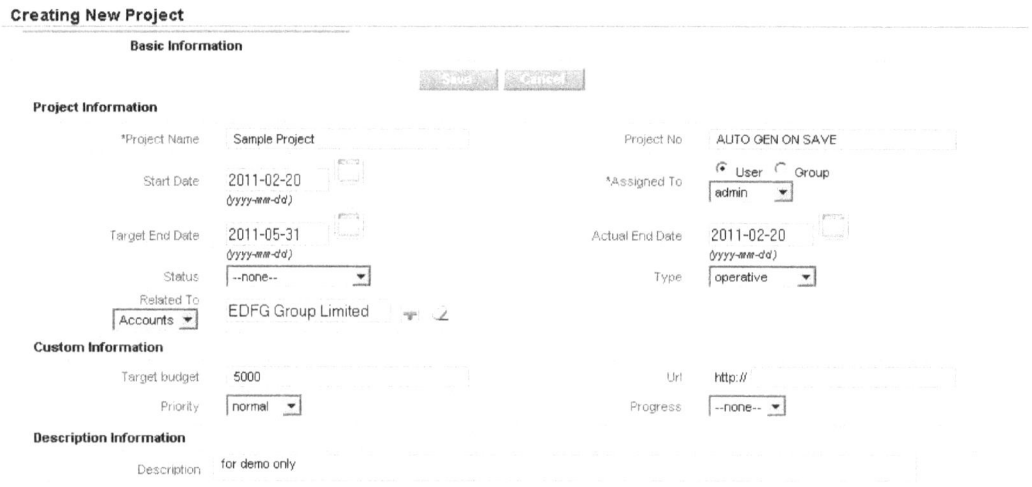

Figure 2-48: Project - Create View - Master Data

Project Information

Table 2-21: Projects - Special default master data entry fields

Entry Field	Description
Project Name:	You have to give each project a unique name.
Project No:	The project number is generated by the CRM automatically based on the CRM administrator's setup. Refer to Section *4.2.4 Other Settings - Customize Record Numbering* for more information.
Start and Target End Date:	Set the time period for the project. This will get considered in the graphical presentation.

Entry Field	Description
Progress:	Set the project progress in %.

Click **[Save]** to transfer your project information to the CRM system. After saving, the detail view of your project opens. You will see the master data you have just entered. If you click the **[More Information]** tab you have now the possibility to link trouble tickets, documents and other related information to the project. You are now ready to add milestones and project tasks.

2.8.2 Project

Each project has milestones. The simplest case is having milestones with a start and an end date only. For larger projects, however, it is recommended that additional milestones be set in order to keep track of the project's development, the resources involved and to compare the project's progress with the original plan.

In order to add milestones to your project, open a project's detail view and click the [More Information] tab. Click the **[Add Project Milestone]** button to enter the Create View of the milestone menu as illustrated in Figure 2-50.

Figure 2-49: Project Milestone - Create View - Master Data

Milestone Information

Table 2-22: Project Milestone - Projects - Special default master data entry fields

Entry Field	Description
Milestone Name:	You have to give each milestone a unique name.
Milestone No:	The milestone number is generated by the CRM automatically based on the CRM administrator's setup. Refer to Section *4.2.4 Other Settings - Customize Record Numbering* for more information.

Entry Field	Description
Related To:	This field links a milestone with a specific project.
Milestone Date:	This is the day on which the milestone becomes valid.

Click **[Save]** to transfer your milestone information to the CRM system. After saving, the detail view of your milestone opens. You may add additional milestones as needed.

2.8.3 Project Tasks

Everything that needs to be done for a project should get collected in separate project tasks. Tasks might be related to a project. Click the ☞ icon to enter a new contract as illustrated in Figure 2-51.

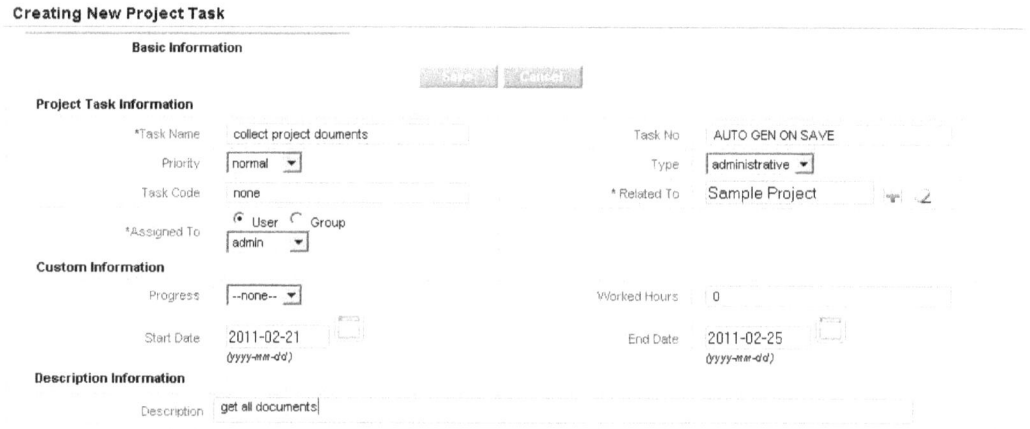

Figure 2-50: Project Task - Create View - Master Data

Click **[Save]** to transfer your project task information to the CRM system. After saving, the detail view of your task opens. You will see the master data you have just entered. If you click the **[More Information]** tab you have the possibility to set relations to documents.

3 Working with the CRM System

This chapter explains how to work efficiently with the CRM system. It includes usage hints within the sales process from a leads stage to after-sales services.

3.1 General Remarks

3.1.1 Working with Lists

If you click appropriate menus in the navigation area, you will see a list of all data stored in the CRM system. Over time, these lists can become very large and difficult to handle. Furthermore, due to limited screen size, only a few columns can be displayed. Therefore, it is appropriate and usually also necessary to adapt the list views to the respective needs of the users. Generally, each user can create individual lists with a specific content and make these lists available for other users. Thus, you have a very effective tool for managing larger data sets, being informed automatically about changes, or selecting data for further use.

Customize Lists

In order to get a list view of data related to your particular interests you may create a custom list view based on the following parameters:

For your customized list view you may define the following parameter:

- the content of the columns (what will be displayed),
- the time interval in which data have been created or changed,
- various logical AND and OR operations between data stored in the CRM system.
- For instance, to create a new list view for organizations, click **[New]** as shown in Figure 3-1. The new window that opens, as shown in Figure 3-2, will give you the opportunity to create your own list view.

Figure 3-1: Create a custom filter for a list view

Individual lists make working with the CRM system much easier. However, mistakes in the list composition, especially by logical AND and OR operations, can lead to unexpected results. Therefore, inexperienced users should begin with simple lists and simple logical filters, and should examine the results carefully

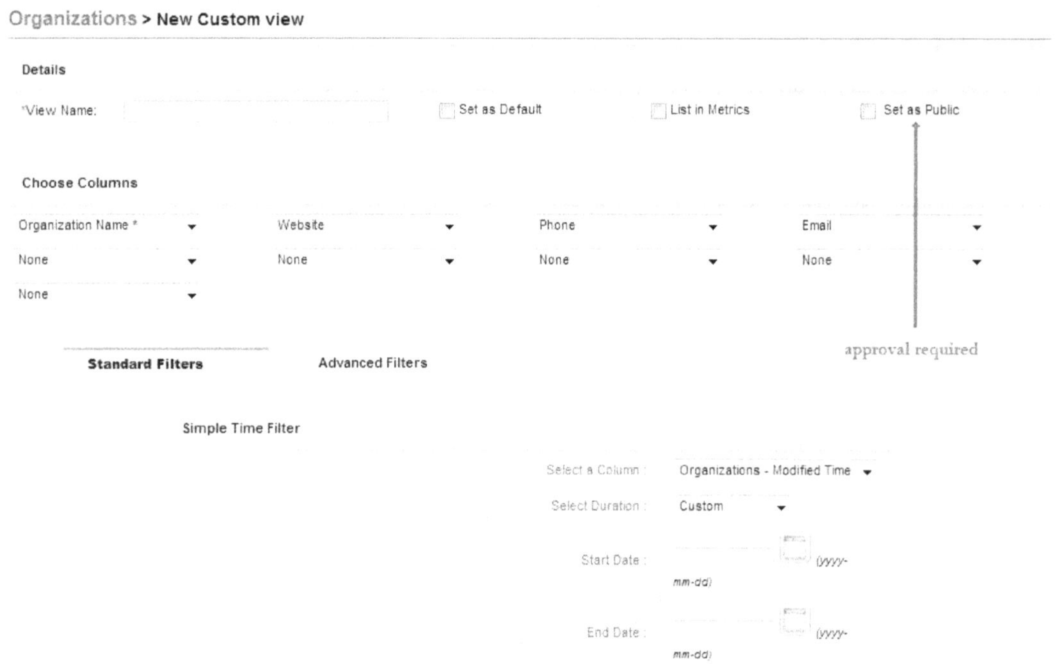

Figure 3-2: Create Custom List - Edit View

For a creation of a new list view the following approach is recommended:

- Enter a short but unique name for your list.
- Select the content of the columns. Keep in mind that the more columns you select the more space on your screen is required. Up to 9 columns are available.
- Set a time filter if required. Set logical AND or OR operations for further filtering your data with the advanced filter menu.

You may change the default list view by selecting the **[Set as Default]** check box. You may also select the created list view to be present at the Key Metrics, located at Home, by marking the **[List in Metrics]** check box.

The functions of the Key Metrics are explained later in this manual section. As a user without admin privileges you will see the list views which have been made public, your own views, your own views which are pending for approval, and the views of other users which are assigned to you by the roles hierarchy.

> You may include check boxes in your advanced filter options. If you want to check whether a check box is marked, use the terms "yes" or "1" for comparison. If you want to have a list of entries with unmarked check boxes use "no" or "0" for comparison.

If you mark the check box **[Set as Public]** your list view will be also be available for other users after review and approval by an user with administration privileges (admin user). The admin user will see your created list view as a pending view as illustrated at Figure 3-3 and will have to approve this view to make it available to all the other CRM users. An admin user is also empowered to reverse the process and deny public access to a custom view. As a user with admin privileges you will see all public, pending and private list views from other users.

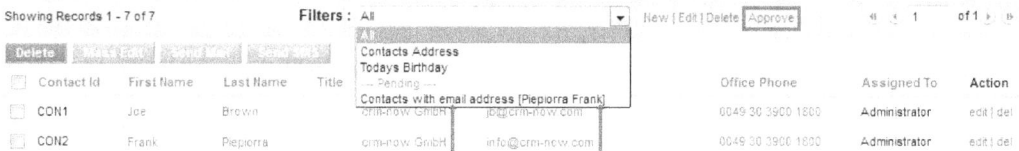

Figure 3-3: Approve Custom View

Record Change Indicator

For each record, the CRM system recognizes the user who changes the content of a record. If this user is different from the user who owns a record (assigned to) the CRM indicates that someone else made modifications by an icon as displayed in Figure 3-4. This icon will disappear automatically as soon the owner of a record reviews the entry.

Figure 3-4: Record Change Indicator

Key Metrics

The Key Metrics view is located on your Home page. It offers a comprehensive view of the most important data stored within your CRM system. This is done by providing a quantitative summary of the information selected by your criteria. The content of the Key Metrics is defined by your custom list views. For an introduction to custom list views, you may look at the description of customize lists in this manual. If the check box **[List in Metrics]** is marked within a list, the CRM will consider this list as part of the Key Metrics. As a result the CRM automatically calculates the data displayed at the Key Metrics.

You may use the Key Metrics to answer questions such as:

- How many quotes are sent to prospect customers?
- How many tickets of a special customer are open?
- How many sales opportunities are in the last stage?

You may have other questions or you may find your own criteria. The possibilities for listings in Key Metrics are limited only by the CRM's capabilities of creating list views. You may use Key Metrics for critical processes, in order to recognize immediately whether something has changed. For instance, a sales person can immediately see if the service team has to solve critical tasks with a special customer; a manager can watch the progress in a sales cycle; a service colleague can see whether the company has won new customers etc.

List Search

If you have many entries in your list views of leads, contacts, organizations etc., a search function helps you to find a specific entry fast. Click the **[magnifying glass icon]** in the list view to open the search display, as shown in the following figure.

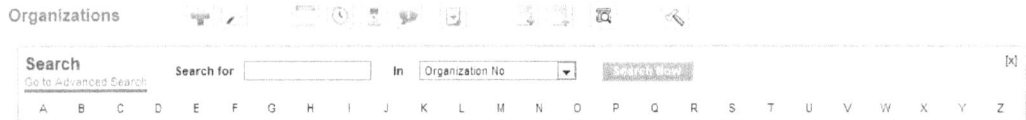

Figure 3-5: List View - Basic Search

The basic search function searches for entries related to the master data.

In addition, you may search by alphabetical order.

Figure 3-6: List View - Advanced Search

If you click **[Go to Advanced Search]**, a new search window will open that allows you a more detailed search based on logical combinations for all fields, as shown in Figure 3-6: List View - Advanced Search. You may add as many search criteria as you need. You may switch between the basic and the advanced search at any time. Click the **[Search]** button to start your search.

Mass Edit In Lists

If you need to change the content of specific fields for a list of entries all at once you may use the mass edit function available in most of the list views. Mark the entries you would like to modify and click the **[Mass Edit]** button. At the new window which opens you may set a new content for your entry fields as illustrated in Figure 3-7.

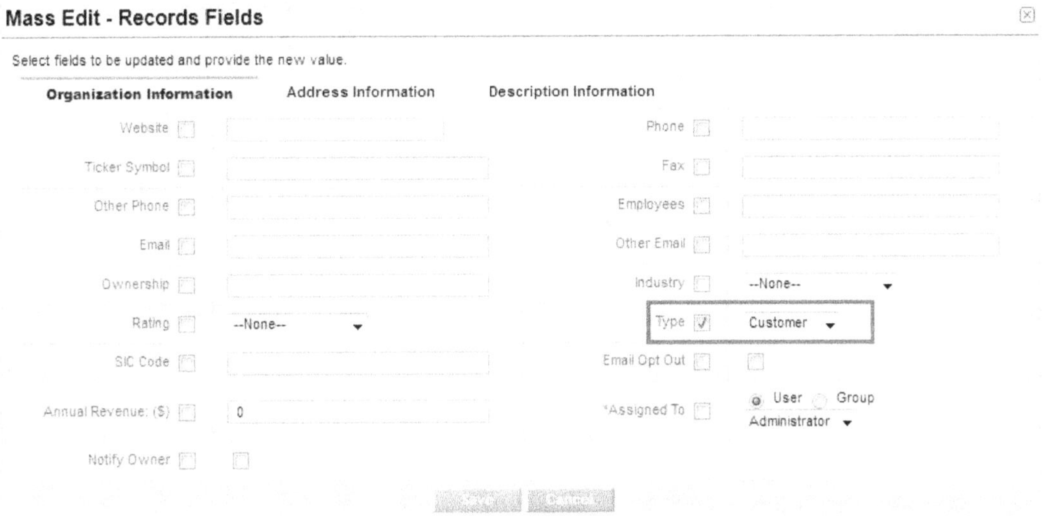

Figure 3-7: List View - Mass Edit

Send E-Mail From Lists

You may send emails from a list view of leads, contacts or organizations to multiple recipients at once by marking the list entries and clicking the **[Send Mail]** button. However,

> To make sure every entry has an email address you may consider this in your custom list view filter by adding the condition (email not equals to <empty>).

you need to make sure in advance that all marked list entries have an email address. If you try to send an email to a list of entries, and one or more do not have an email address, there will be no warning message.

Mailer Export From Lists

Sometimes you may need email or address data from contacts or organizations for purposes not covered by the CRM system's functionality. By clicking the **[Mailer Export]** button at the contact's or organization's list view the CRM provides a convenient function to export such information as a text file with comma separated values (CSV) as illustrated in Figure 3-8.

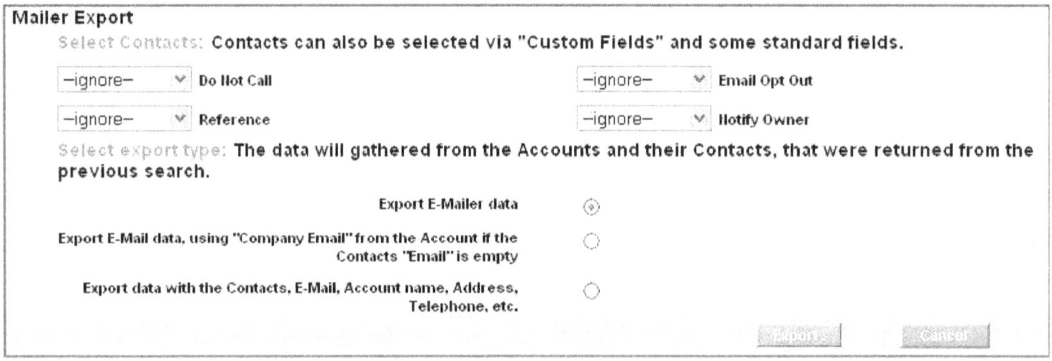

Figure 3-8: List View - Mailer Export

The character format of the exported file is UTF-8 as it is used by the CRM internally. For further use with other applications you may convert UTF-8 characters to any other character format.

Remove Duplicate Entries

Data duplicates are dangerous for the CRM usage. Imagine you have entered for instance the same contact twice and one of your sale staff is using the first entry while the other sales representatives are working with the second entry. Since both contact entries do not relate to each other, your sales staff does not get valid information about the contact's history or future plans.

To prevent duplicates in some cases the CRM checks for already-existing entries. For instance, if you try to enter a new organization with an organization name which already exist you will get a warning message.

However, the CRM software can't avoid duplicates completely. For instance, you may get duplicates from data imports or synchronization (e.g. Outlook Plugin) or by users with different access privileges.

In order to remove duplicates, the CRM provides a function in the list views to find duplicates for leads, contacts, organizations, opportunities, products, tickets and vendors. Click the search duplicate icon at the list view to open the duplicate search menu as illustrated in Figure 3-10.

The icon is not available for custom views. Select from the available fields menu your search criteria and hit the **[Find Duplicates]** button.

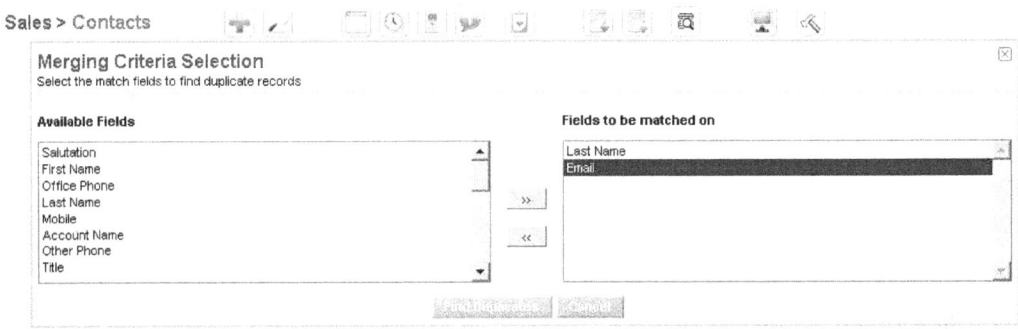

Figure 3-10: List View - Duplicate Search

The opening menu displays all records which are identified as duplicates and allows you to delete entries or to merge the content of duplicate records as shown in Figure 3-9.

You may merge up to 3 records. The entity type column indicates the source of a record.

	recordid	Last Name	Email	Entity Type	Merge Select	Action
☐	22	Smith	mary_smith@company.com	Existing	☐	
☐	24	Smith	mary_smith@company.com	Existing	☐	

Select the records you want to merge and hit the **Merge** button. A new window pops up

Figure 3-9: Duplicate Search Result

which displays the content of the records as shown in Figure 3-11.

First select the record you want to keep as the primary record. Then mark the content of the fields you want to add to the primary record. You should direct your special attention to the **Assigned To** field. If you merge picklist entries which are only accessible by users with administration privileges these entries will be displayed as "not accessible" to users which do not have administration privileges. Hit the **[Merge]** button to finish the process. Your primary record will be updated and the other records will be moved to the recycle bin.

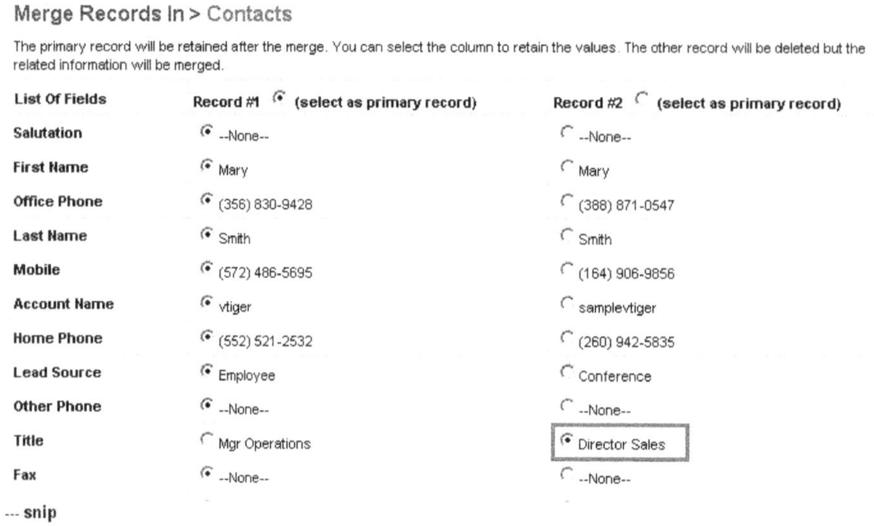

![Merge Records screenshot]

Figure 3-11: Duplicate Merge and Removal

3.1.2 Tag Cloud

Tag Clouds are designed to improve the usability of the CRM. They help you categorize CRM entries based on the user's judgment or rating, independent from categories set by the CRM system.

Tag Clouds are based on the assumption that humans tend to pool objects based on subjective or other values. Such a pooling is in fact a new categorization of data stored in the CRM system. To meet such a requirement for categorization, the Tag Clouds provide users the capability to build categories which are not limited to a single CRM module. These categories are independent from the categories defined at the master data of each CRM entry, usually the pick list entries.

For instance, a sales person may consider a meeting, a customer and a service request as **important**. These new categories or groups can be defined freely. You may use any terms such as **important**, **Proposal, Berlin**, **private** or **Spring**. You may add such a term with the **[Tag it]** button to any CRM entry that can be considered to be in the same category.

Figure 3-12: Tag Cloud

A tag cloud entry is shown in Figure 3-12. The more CRM entries are labeled with the same tag, the bigger this tag will be displayed in the tag cloud.

> Tags are always single words! Do not use sentences or combined expressions.

Use the term listed in the Tag Cloud to find all CRM entries which have the same tag. On the Home page, all tags will be displayed. Tags for a corresponding entity will only be displayed in the detail view. On clicking the tag, in both the detail view and the Home page, the entities tagged with the corresponding tag will be displayed. You can delete the tag from the detail view tag cloud. You can also delete a tag by deleting the entity.

To delete a tag, move your mouse pointer above the tag word. An "x" icon will appear. Click this icon to delete the tag. Alternatively you can delete your data entry. With this entry the tag will also be deleted.

Tag cloud entries are assigned to the user who made the entry. You can't share tag cloud entries with other users. If a user does not intend to use the tag cloud this function can be switched off as explained in Section 1.3.4.

3.1.3 Calendar Reminder Popup

Each user can activate an activity reminder function by setting a reminder interval at the **[My Preferences]** menu as explained in Section 1.3.4 - *My Preferences*. If activated, a popup browser window will be displayed every time an activity is due. The popup window displays the time, status, and subject of an activity. It offers you the option to postpone or to close a reminder message. If postponed, the message will pop up again after the next reminder interval until it is closed.

3.1.4 Chat Functions

The chat functions offered by the CRM system provide instant messaging capabilities in a form of real-time communication between two or more CRM users based on typed text. The CRM system offers public as well as a private chat capability in so-called chat rooms. The public chat allows all CRM users to share a common chat room where each user can read all messages and can contribute if desired. The private chat room serves as a platform for the communications between two users. To open a chat room click the **[Chat]** icon, as it is available at every list view. A new browser window will open, as illustrated in Figure 3-13.

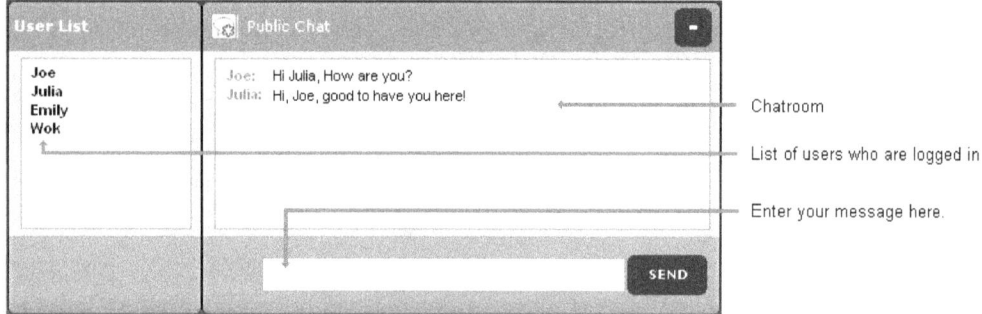

Figure 3-13: Chat View

To contribute to the chat, enter your message and click **[Send]**. Your message will be displayed at the chat room. Besides the chat room, you see the list of logged-in users. To open a private chat, click the appropriate user name.

3.1.5 Tools Menu

The CRM offers a set of additional tools which are useful for the daily work with customers.

RSS

RSS is a Web feed format, used for Web syndication and stands for Really Simple Syndication. Web feeds are widely used by the web community for sharing the latest entries headlines or their full text, and even attach multimedia files. Some providers allow other websites to incorporate their syndicated headline or headline and short summary feeds. RSS is used for many purposes, including marketing, bug-reports, or any other activity involving periodic updates or publications. Many corporations are turning to RSS for delivering their news, replacing email and fax distribution. The news media is also utilizing RSS by bypassing traditional news sources CRM. Users are able to have news constantly fed to them instead of searching for them.

In the **[RSS]** menu the CRM system provides an RSS reader - which can check a list of feeds on behalf of the users and displays any updated articles that it finds. You may search the Web for RSS feeds you are interested in. Every RSS feed has a unique address similar to Web URLs. To watch an RSS feed, you have to enter these addresses into the CRM system.

My Sites

You may link the CRM system with other web sites which are of any interest to your business. Users do not need to leave the CRM system to access third party web sites or other Intranet or Internet sites. You may use this function, for instance, for watching important customers, your own web site, or the websites of your competitors. It is also very useful for tracking shipments, or conducting web-based communication with vendors.

Before you can see any website at the **[My Site]** menu, you need to bookmark a site. Click **[Manage Sites]** to enter a new web site. Click the **[My Sites]** to see the bookmarked web sites.

Documents

Documents are practical to add further information to CRM entries. You may enter a document by using the **Quick-Menu** or the icon at the list view of the **[Documents]** menu. You may also add documents directly at the detail views of certain CRM modules. As displayed in Figure 3-14 the CRM comes with a default document folder setup and you may add additional folders if required. Note that empty folders are hidden from the view and the Move button is only available to the CRM administrator.

Figure 3-14: Documents - Default Folder

In the **[Documents]** menu click the icon to create a new document as shown in Figure 3-15. You need to give the document a unique name and to select the folder in which the document is going to be saved. The create view allows you to enter three different document types:

- **Text:** Use the editor at the **Description** field to enter your information.
- **File:** At the **Download Type** field select **Internal** and browse at your computer or network for the file you want to upload to the CRM. Such a file will be available for download from the CRM as long the check box for **[Active]** is switched to **yes**
- **External Source:** At the **Download Type** field select **External** and enter the Web or LAN address (URL) of your files.

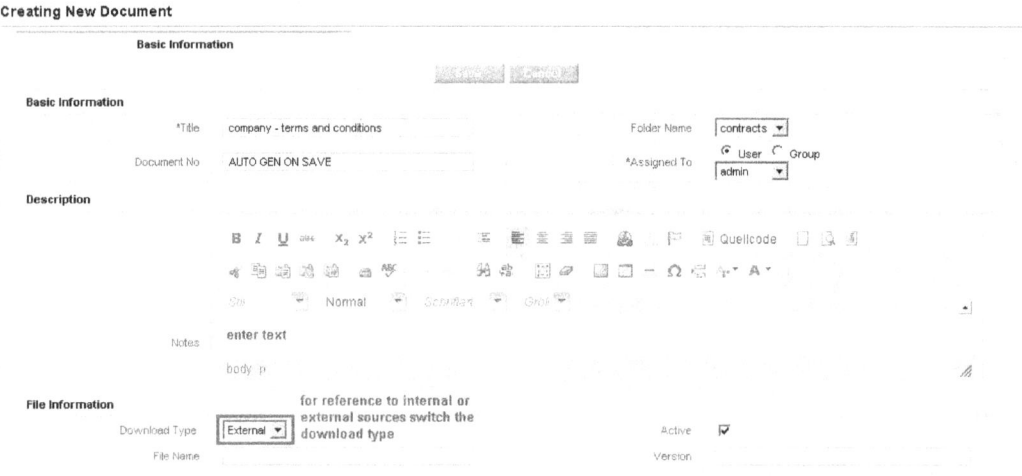

Figure 3-15: Documents - Create View

Recycle Bin

This menu is only available if you have installed the appropriate optional CRM package. In most cases it is not recommended to delete any data from the CRM. If you do it unintentionally, the deleted data may be restored from the recycle bin.

Open the **Recycle Bin** menu as illustrated in Figure 3-16 and select the CRM module for which would like to restore deleted data. Then all deleted records will be displayed. You are only allowed to restore the data if you have proper permissions. You may restore records either individually or multiple records at once but only within the selected module. When a record from particular module gets restored, also all the related records from other modules are restored automatically if possible.

The CRM administrator is empowered to empty the recycle bin and to remove the deleted entries from the CRM system permanently. Note that removed data can't get recovered anymore.

Figure 3-16: Recycle Bin - List View

3.1.6 Send and Receive Emails

The CRM system offers a variety of methods for including email in your work with your customers, co- workers, suppliers and other contacts.

You may

send emails to contacts, organizations or leads directly from the CRM system:
>These functions are explained in the following as Send Emails and Email Mass Mailing.

transfer received or sent emails from your office environment to the CRM system:
>The CRM comes with an Outlook plugin as well as a Thunderbird/Mozilla email client extension. You may use these additional programs on your computer.

receive emails at the CRM system from personal mail account
>The functions offered to receive emails are explained in the following as Receiving Emails

For outgoing emails you have to configure a common mail server access as explained in section *4.2.4 Other Settings - Outgoing Server*. You will also need to configure the access to the individual receiving mail servers for each individual user as explained later in this section.

3.1.6.1 Send Emails

If you want to use the CRM system for outgoing emails you have the following options:

- You may create an email from the Detail View of one of your leads, contacts or organizations. By using the contact details already stored at your CRM system, the system makes sure that the sent emails will be stored in reference to the existing contact entries.
- You may create an email from the List View.
- You may create an email directly at the Emails menus **Mail Manager** or its

predecessor **Email**, previously called Webmail. In this case the reference to a contact has to be made manually. Both modules are explained in Section 3.1.6.3.

Note the special **Access Count** column at the email reference list at a Contact's Detail View. Here you may see whether your email was read by the recipient. This information gets available by a little invisible 1x1 pixel image sent with every email from the CRM. If a recipient opens the email with an email client set to allow the display of images in emails, the display of the little image will get counted in the CRM.

3.1.6.2 Send Email Mass Mailing

You may send a common email from the CRM to several people at the same time from a List View or Campaign. You may use this function for mass mailings to your customers or to other contacts stored in your CRM system.

- Create a custom view of your leads, contacts, or organizations. Use the filter operations to select the desired contacts.
- Save the custom view.
- Display the custom view. Select the contacts which are going to receive your mass mailing. Click the **[Send Mail]** button at the bottom of the list to call the Email menu as shown in Figure 3-17.

Figure 3-17: Mass Mailing Selection

The CRM system can store your standard email signature and add it to your email message automatically. The signature is set at the **[My Preferences]** menu at the CRM's Management Area or by the CRM administrator.

The email creation window will open as shown in Figure 3-18. Edit your email. You may also add further email addresses which you have not selected before.

Click the **[Send]** button to send your email immediately, or the **[Save]** button, to store the email at the CRM system without sending it. With the **[Select Email Template]** button you may pick an email template which you have created before.

The menu is explained in the following tables. Note the special behavior of the **To** field.

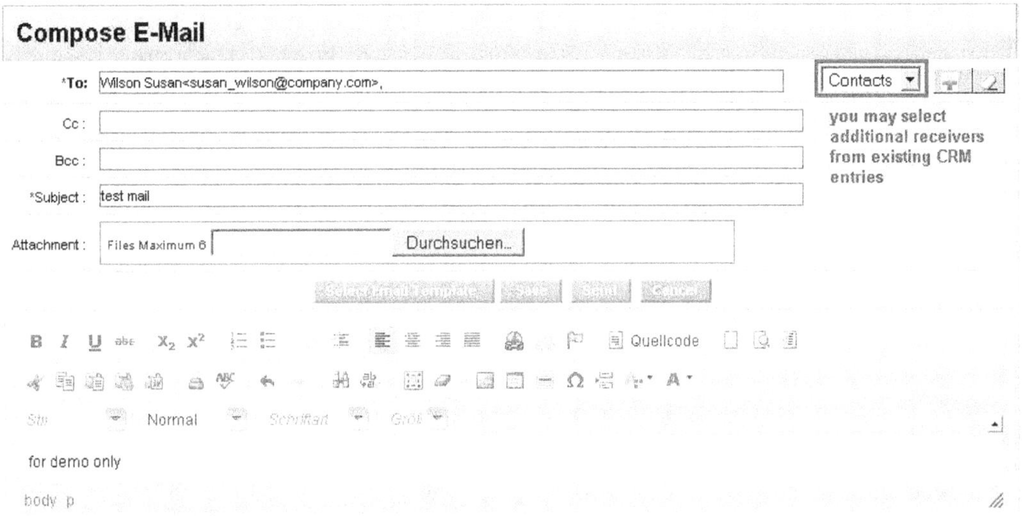

Figure 3-18: Compose Email Menu

Table 3-1: Outgoing Emails - Common entry fields

Field	Description
To:	Here you may enter the email addresses of the recipients. Each recipient will receive a separate email and will not be able to see other recipients if you have sent the email to multiple recipients.
CC:	CC stands for Carbon Copy. The recipient entered here will receive a copy of the sent mail. The CC recipient will be also visible to all recipients listed in the **To** field.
BCC:	BCC stands for Blind Carbon Copy. This means the same as CC, however the recipients entered here will be not visible for the other email recipients.
Attachment	You may add an attachment to your email. At the current release maximum size of an attachment is limited to a file size of about 1 MB but can get changed by the CRM administrator.

Table 3-2: Outgoing Emails - Special supporting buttons

Field	Description
Select Email Template:	The CRM offers you to work with email templates. These templates must be designed and stored at the CRM system as explained in CRM administration section.
Send:	The email will be sent. A signature will be added automatically if defined before. The email will be assigned to the sending user. A copy of the email will be automatically sent by the CRM system to the assigned user.
Save	You may save this email without sending it. The email will be stored and be listed at the recipient's detail view.

A reference to a copy of the sent emails will be stored at each individual contact and is displayed at the Detail View.

3.1.6.3 Receiving Emails

If you generally receive your email at your office, you may use the Outlook Plugin or the Thunderbird extension to transfer selected emails to the contacts stored in your CRM system.

In addition, you have the possibility to receive emails directly in the CRM. Before you can receive any email at your CRM, you must have set up the access to your receiving email server. As a necessary precondition for this, the user must have access to an email server outside of the CRM system.

Mail Manager Menu

The Mail Manager is the successor of the Webmail module, which is still available as the separate Email module. Before you can use it you need to configure the SMTP server for all outgoing emails, as explained in Section 4.2.4.3, and the user's individual IMAP server access for all incoming mails.

For the IMAP server setup click **Settings** and select your account type as illustrated in Figure 3-19.

vtiger CRM v5.4.x

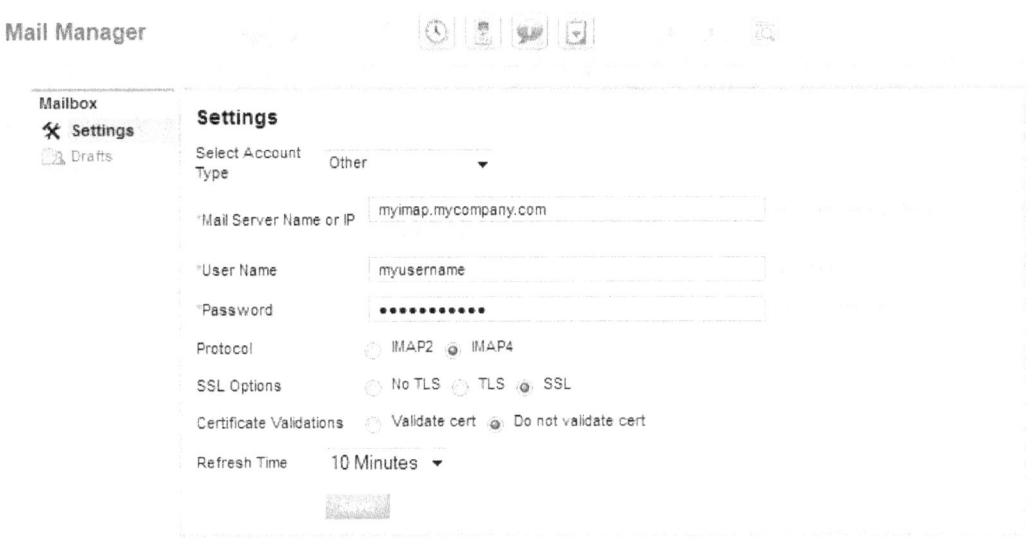

Figure 3-19: Mail Manager - IMAP Settings

Ask your IMAP service provider for the settings details. As soon you click the **[Save]** button the CRM tries to connect to the server. If you get an error message check your server settings. If the settings are correct you will see the existing IMAP folders, as illustrated in Figure 3-20.

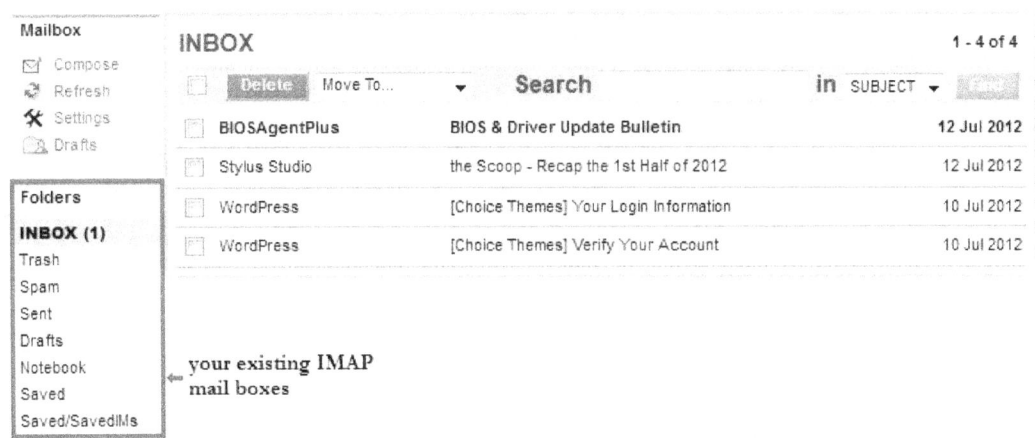

Figure 3-20: Mail Manager - Menu

Click a message to see the details as illustrated in Figure 3-21.

Figure 3-21: Mail Manager - Message Detail View

If the sender's contact is already stored at the CRM you will see a link to the related CRM entry at the **Related Records** menu. If not, you may add the sender's credentials as Contact, Lead or Organization or you may add a ToDo or Ticket.

For the creation of a new email, click **[Compose]**. The new Window which opens is illustrated in Figure 3-22.

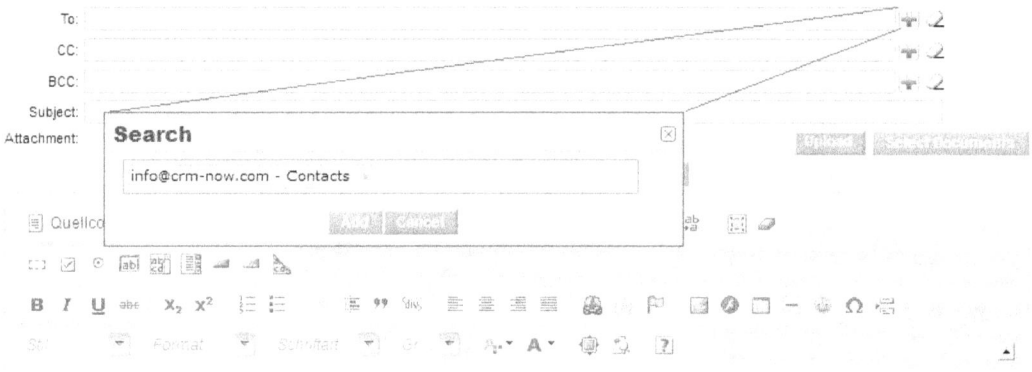

Figure 3-22: Mail Manager - Compose Menu

You may enter your recipient's email addresses directly or search for existing CRM entries by clicking the icon. The search function will look up the CRM's data while you are typing a first or last name.

Note, that each recipient listed in the **To** field gets an individual mail and will not be able to see who else got this email.

Email Menu

Email is the 'old' CRM email client previously called Webmail. It has found its successor in the Mail Manager and complements its functionality. To configure the access to the receiving mail server click **[Email]** menu at the navigation area. You do not need administrative privileges for this operation. The email client menu opens, as shown at Figure 3-23.

Figure 3-23: Email Menu

Click the **[Incoming Mail Server Settings]** icon to open the email server configuration menu as shown in Figure 3-24: Incoming Mail Server Details.

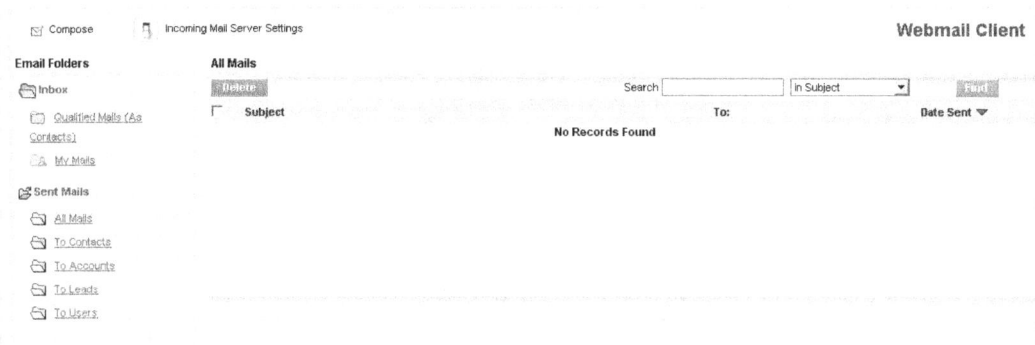

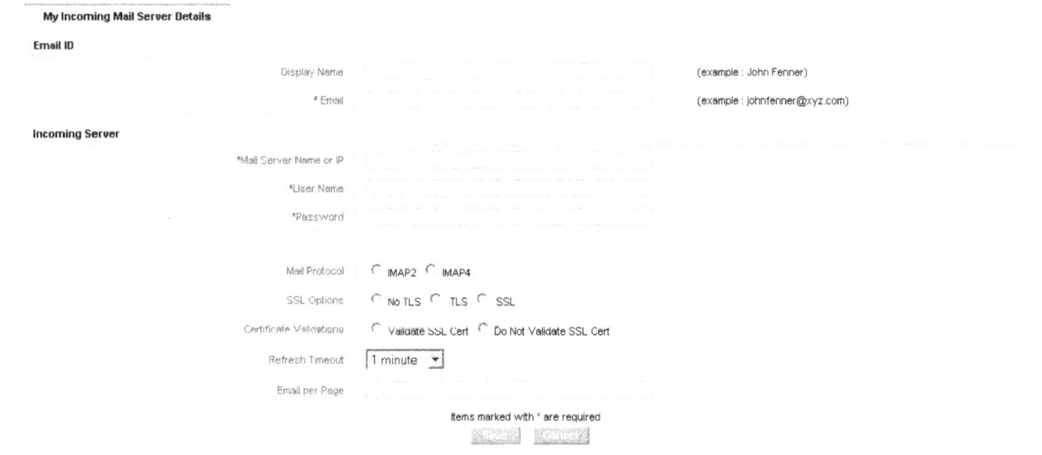

Figure 3-24: Incoming Mail Server Details

You have to enter all configuration data as described in the following table. Please ask your email service provider for the necessary access information.

Table 3-3: Incoming Mail Server Settings Fields

Entry Field	Description
Display Name:	You should give each mail server a unique name. This name will be displayed at the mail server account list.
Email	You must enter the email address you use at your receiving mail server.
Mail Server Settings - Mail Server Name or IP:	You must enter the address of your mail server. You may use a name or the IP address but you have to use a server which supports the IMAP protocol.
Mail Server Settings - User Name	You must enter the user name and the password you use to access the mail server.
Mail Server Settings - Mail Protocol:	In the current version, only IMAP is supported and fully functional as your email protocol. The POP protocol may be available in the future.
Mail Server Settings - SSL Options:	You must select whether you want encrypted communication with your email server.
Mail Server Settings - Certificate Validations:	If you use encryption to access the mail server, you should select whether the certificate is validated.
Mail Server Settings - Use Internal Mailer:	If configured by your service provider, you might use the internal mailer to send emails.
Mail Server Settings - Refresh Timeout:	You may change the refresh rate.
Mail Server Settings - Emails per page:	You may select the number of email you want to display on a single page.

Click **[Save]** to configure the mail function at the CRM system. All your emails are organized at **[Email]** menu as they are organized at your mail server.

The buttons at the top of Figure 3-23 provide the following functions:

Compose:

This opens the compose window.

Settings:

This opens the settings window for your incoming emails. Note that the administrator configures the outgoing mail server.

The CRM comes with a set of standard mail folders:

Inbox:

This folder lists all your incoming emails. Thereby, the following cases are distinguished:

- If an email comes from a contact which is not related to any of the campaigns, on qualifying the email will automatically be moved to the **Qualified Mails** folder and related to that contact.
- If an email comes from an undefined user, on qualifying the CRM system will create a new contact and associates the email to the newly created contact.
- If an email comes from a lead of a Campaign, on qualifying the email of the corresponding Lead will be converted to a contact related with the Campaign. The CRM system traces the conversion ratio of Leads to Contacts on a per campaign basis to judge the effectiveness of a Campaign.
- If an email comes from a Contact of a Campaign, on qualifying the email will be added and related to that Contact.

An email is received in unprotected mode. That means that the CRM does not check for any viruses or other threats frequently transmitted by email. Even though these threats can not cause any damage to the CRM, it is advised to take protective action at the receiving mail server, especially if you plan to download email content to your computer.

Sent Mails:

This folder lists all your sent mails organized by the type of contact.

You may search your emails by subject, sender, or both.

3.2 Working with the sales process

The CRM system has been designed to support you in all phases of the sales cycle, from leads to closed business, by integrating all relevant data. Sales processes are defined differently in each enterprise, yet there are common principles for the work flow, which the CRM system represents. The most common scenario for goods or services with longer sales cycles could be:

- When you have your first contact with a prospective customer, create a lead. At this time you may not know whether this contact has serious interest in the goods or services your company offers. You may collect as much information about this contact as possible.

- Now sales activity will be starting with this lead. You may schedule meetings, make some calls or send emails until you know whether there is a business opportunity.

- If you find out that this lead does not go any further, you set the lead status to lost and forget about it. If this lead looks promising for your business, you can convert it to a sales opportunity.

- During conversion the CRM will create a sales opportunity, an organization and a contact, using the data you have already collected. The lead will be deleted.

- Now you start working with the opportunity. You indicate the progress by setting different sales stages.

The contact and organizations information related to your sales opportunity are the foundation for you and your co- workers to build a relationship with a potential customer. You may use this information for scheduling and controlling activities, distributing tasks, forecasting revenues, understanding the purchase decision process of a customer, and much more.

3.2.1 Working with Leads

A lead represents the first stage of the sales process and is therefore the starting point for many activities. In order to work with leads effectively the CRM system provides a set of tools.

Leads List View

You may reach the lead list view at the **[Sales] > [Leads]** menu as shown in Figure 3-25: Lead List View.

Figure 3-25: Lead List View

At this menu you may

- **delete leads:** Mark the leads to be deleted and hit the appropriate button.
- **send emails to leads:** Mark the leads to be recipients and hit the appropriate button.
- **edit multiple entries at once:** Mark the leads to be changed and hit the appropriate button.
- **create, modify and use display filters:** As described in section 3.1.1 Working with Lists, you may change the content of your list view on the basis of filters.
- **merge lead information with email templates:** Mark the leads to be merged, select a template and hit the appropriate button.

Link Leads with other CRM entries

You may link a lead with other activities such as calls, meetings or tasks and with emails, attachments, notes or products. To establish such links, you may use one of the following methods:

- **By the lead detail view:** Open an existing lead and create new entries related to this lead at the **[More Information]** tab.

- **By direct entry:** Click **[New Event]**, **[New Task]**, **[New Note]** or **[New Product]** in the entry area of your CRM system, or open an existing entry. Select the related Lead as a reference before you save your entries. The information will be linked to the lead and will be available at the lead's detail view.

All established links will be also available at sales opportunities after conversion as explained in Section 2.3.2.

3.2.2 Working with Opportunities

In the sales process, opportunities are the logical successors to leads. Therefore, you should create a sales opportunity from a lead and transfer all information available for the lead to this sales opportunity as explained in the next section. You can also create a sales opportunity directly.

Sales opportunities are characterized by the contact having shown obvious interest in your company's offering. Your sales department expects that an offer can be made in the future and estimates that it is appropriate to take over lead data.

Creating Opportunities from Leads

To create a sales opportunity based on an existing lead, you must switch to the lead detail

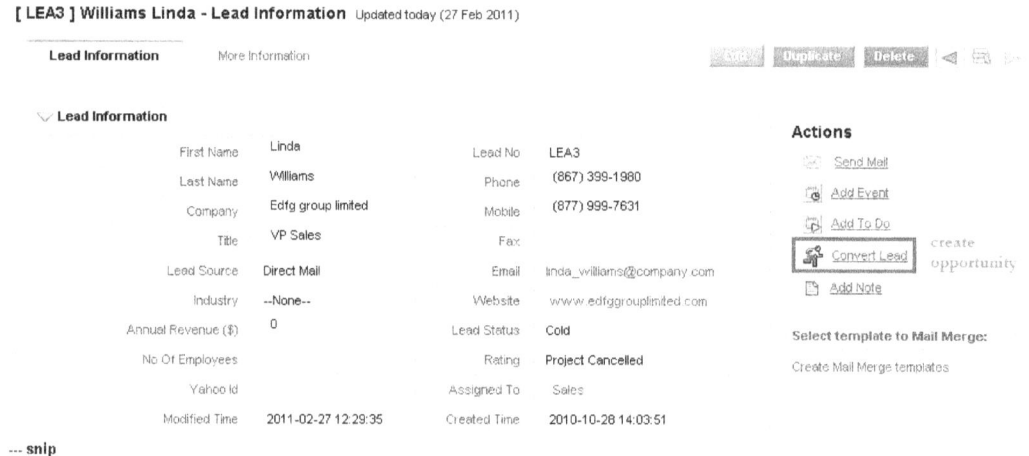

Figure 3-26: Lead Detail View - Master Data

view as shown in Figure 3-26.

Click the link **[Convert Lead]**. A new pop up window will open as shown in Figure 3-27.

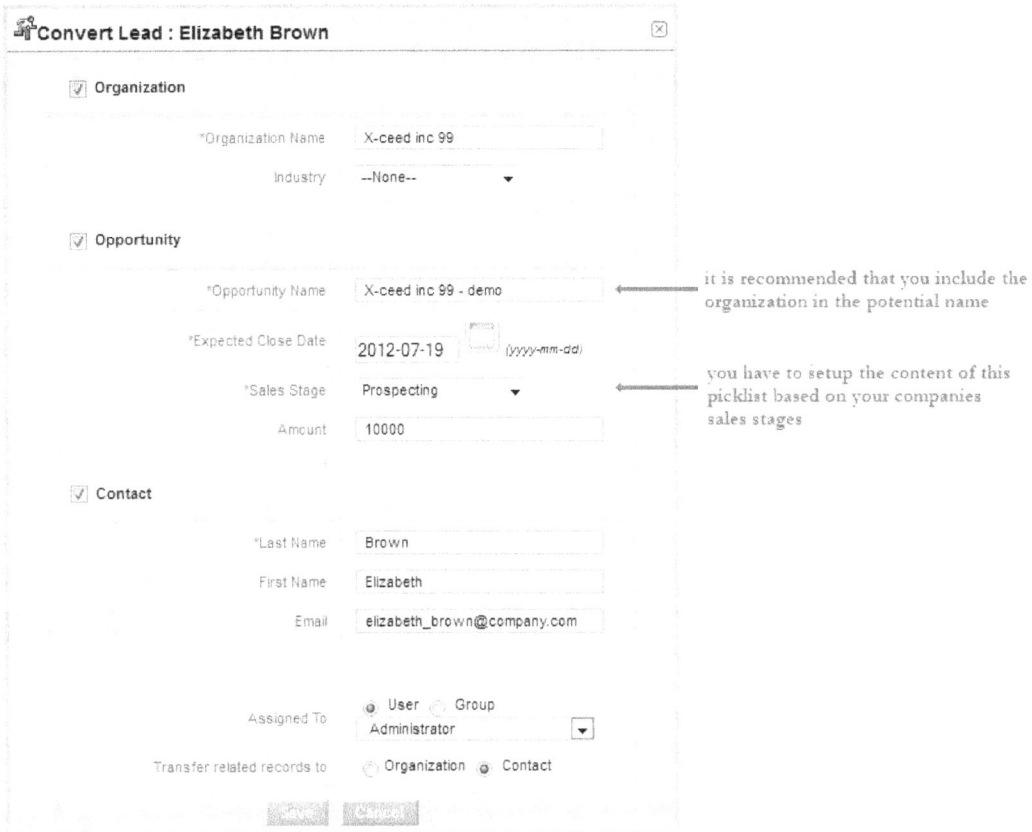

Figure 3-27: Convert leads menu

With the lead conversion, the following operations can be performed automatically by the CRM system:

Creation of a new opportunity.

- Creation of new entries for **Opportunity**, **Organizations** and **Contacts** and linking all to each other.
- Transfer of all data from the lead to the new created entries. Note, that related records as you have stored at the **More Information** tab at Leads, will get moved to the **More Information** tab at Organizations or Contacts but not to both.
- Assignment of the created organization, contact and opportunity to the selected user or group.
- Deletion of the lead.

In reference to the Figure 3-27, you can control the conversion as explained in the following table.

A lead transformation cannot get reversed.

Table 3-1: List of settings for lead conversion

Field Entry	Description
Assigned To:	Here you may choose a new owner for the converted data.
Organization Name and Industry:	This shows you the organization name and industry for the new CRM organization entry. The content comes from the lead's entry.
Opportunity:	If you unmark this check box, only entries for an organization and for a contact can get created by the conversion. There will be no opportunity related to it. You may use this function if you intend to store organization and/or contact information which is not related to an upcoming business but important enough to be listed in the CRM.
Opportunity Name:	Here you must enter a unique name for your new opportunity. It makes sense to include the organization name in order to maintain a clear name structure.
Opportunity Close Date:	Pick a likely closing date for this potential business. You will be able to change it later if necessary. This is particularly useful information for creating forecasts.
Opportunity Amount:	You may enter an amount of the business you expect. You may change it later. This amount may be used for forecasts.
Opportunity Sales Stage:	You must enter a sales stage for the opportunity. The sales stages can be defined and changed by the CRM administrator.

Click **[Save]** to execute the conversion.

After conversion, the browser content will switch to the detail view of the organization you have just created. At the **More Information** tab you will also find the links to the related contact and the sales opportunity. Your new opportunity is now also listed at the List View as shown in Figure 3-28.

Figure 3-28: Opportunities List View

Change the Opportunities List View

You may reach the lead list view at the **[Opportunities]** menu as shown at the previous figure. At this menu you may:

- **delete opportunities:** Mark the opportunities to be deleted and hit the appropriate button.
- **edit multiple entries at once:** Mark the opportunities to be changed and hit the appropriate button.
- **create, modify and use display filters:** You may change the content of your list view on the basis of filters.
- **search lists:** As describes in section 3.1.1, you may reduce the number of opportunities displayed by using the filters of the advanced search function

Use the Opportunity Detail View

You may reach an opportunities' detail view by clicking an opportunities' name at the list view. You may use this view to link an opportunity with further CRM information which is important for your customer relationship. At the **[More Information]** tab you are provided with a large variety of possibilities for linking an opportunity with other CRM records. This is the right place to enter any activities, documents, or other information related to your sales process. Each time you reach a new sales stage an automatic entry at the Sales Stage History will be made.

Send Emails to Contacts related to Opportunities

In order to send an email to a contact which is listed at the opportunities' detail view, you need to select this contact by clicking its name. The detail view of this contact opens. Proceed as described in *Section: Sending Emails*. You may send an email to multiple contacts by creating a special list and using the mass mail function as explained in *Section: Email Mass Mailing*.

Link Opportunities with other CRM Entries

You may link an opportunity with other activities such as calls, meetings or tasks and with contacts, products, attachments, notes, quotes or sales orders. To establish such links you may use one of the following methods:

1. **by the opportunity detail view**

    Open an existing opportunity and create new entries related to this opportunity.

2. **by direct entry**

Click **[New Event]**, **[New Task]**, **[New Notes]**, **[New Quote]** or **[New Sales Order]** at the entry area of your CRM system, or open an existing entry. Select the related opportunity as a reference before saving your entries. The information will be linked to the opportunity and will be available at the detail view.

3.2.3 Working with Support

The CRM system offers extensive functionality to maintain the valuable customer relationships after sales. Why should you use the support functions?

- Above all, the support functions help you to collect and sort customer requests, inquiries and disturbances, problems etc. related to sold goods or services.
- The support functions keep CRM users and customers informed on the status reached in respect to the response to customer's messages.
- Support staff has a very effective tool to keep track of customer complaints or requirements related to customers or products or both.
- Sales staff and management can get a quick overview of support activities related to customers or products or both.
- CRM users or customers have convenient access to frequently asked questions (FAQ). This can help your company keep the service requests low and maintain standard procedures in responding to customer's requests.

The CRM's capabilities to provide FAQ as well as tickets are extended by the Customer Portal functions as explained in the Customer Portal manual.

Trouble Tickets

In CRM terminology, tickets are any kind of customer service requests as they occur after sales. Tickets are listed at the **[Trouble Tickets]** menu.

Create New Tickets

To create a new ticket, open the **[Trouble Tickets]** menu. You may use the magnifying glass icon on top of the list for searching the list. You may also use this menu to change the content of a single or multiple tickets at once, delete unwanted tickets, set filter functions for the list view or merge ticket information with templates.

Click the ✱ icon to open a new ticket as shown at Figure 3-29.

Figure 3-29: Trouble Ticket - Edit View

You should enter as much information as possible. Use the Priority, Severity and Category to weight the ticket. Your CRM system administrator may add additional custom fields to your tickets or change the content of the drop down lists.

Table 3-4: Trouble Tickets - Special default entry fields

Entry Field	Description
Assigned To:	You may assign the ticket to a person who is listed as CRM user or to a user group. This user or group will be in charge to answer to the customer's request and will be notified by email about any changes to a ticket.
Title:	You should give each ticket a unique name.
Contacts, Organizations:	If you link a ticket to a specific contact or organization and you have not disabled the automatic email distribution for such a contact or organization an email will be send to the related contact automatically any time the content of the ticket changes.
Hours, Days:	If you link the ticket to a service contract this information is used to calculate the content of the total time amount field at the related service contract.

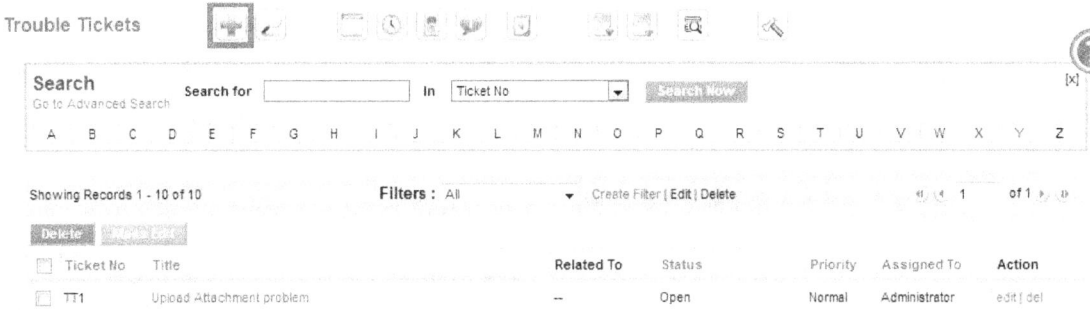

Figure 3-30: Trouble Ticket - List View

Work with Tickets

In Figure 3-31 one sample ticket is already listed. To work with a ticket click its title. A new window will open as shown in the following figure.

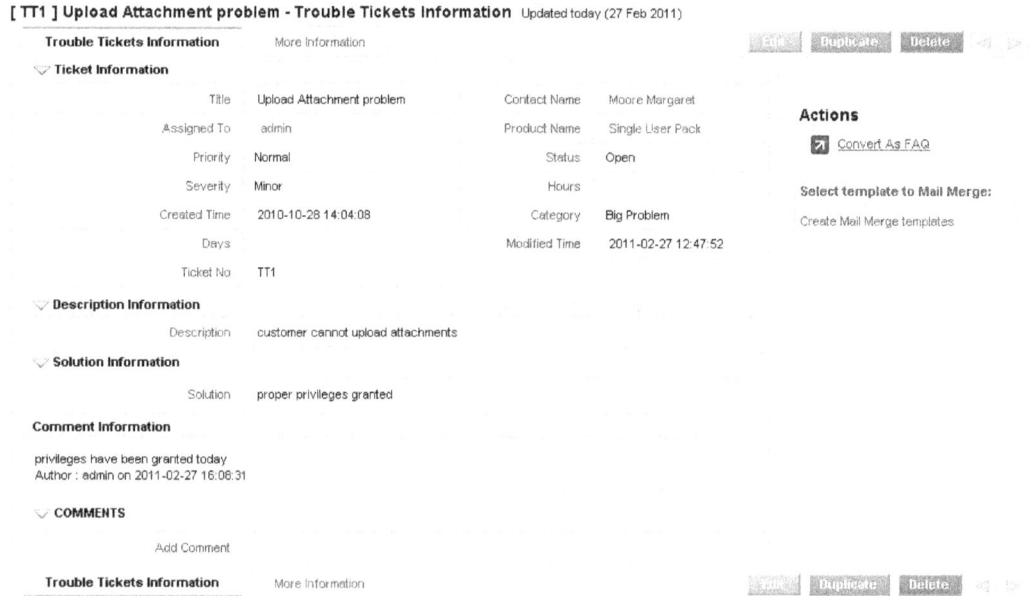

Figure 3-31: Trouble Ticket - Detail View - Master Data

At this menu you may:

- **edit, duplicate or delete a ticket:** The edit function allows you and your co-workers to change the entries and to make comments before or after a solution has been found. Note that you may enter data without opening the edit view. Just move the mouse pointer to the appropriate fields within the detail view to make your entries. With the duplicate function you may copy a ticket. This function might be useful to split ticket. Use the delete function carefully. It might be better to keep a ticket in the list and change its status.

- **convert as FAQ:** You may receive frequent customer requests to a same topic. This function allows you to convert a ticket to a FAQ as explained in the next section.

- **add a tag:** You may use this function to set your own priorities as explained in section: Tag Cloud.

- **merge the ticket information with a template:** You may use this function to merge ticket information with an email template.

You may modify the master data in the edit view of a ticket. Each ticket can go through different working stages and will be closed sooner or later. The CRM will help you to keep track of the working progress and records the changes. Any CRM user can post a comment. The comments will be sorted in chronological order and indicate the CRM user who made the comment. At the end of the life cycle of a ticket, you may present the solution.

All changes to a ticket are displayed at the ticket history. The information provided allows you to find out:

- Who changed the ticket information?
- What changes have been made?
- What was the time line of changes?

Click the **[More Information]** tab to view or to add ticket related activities, documents or services.

If you have the ticket related to a contact or organization, be aware that every time you make changes to the ticket information an automatic email will be sent to the related entry, informing the contact regarding the changes. If you do not want such an email notification to be sent out you have to set the field (check box) **Email Opt out** of the related entry to **yes**.

Frequently Asked Questions (FAQ)

The CRM system can help you create FAQ list. FAQ refers to listed questions and answers, all supposed to be frequently asked in some context, and pertaining to a particular issue. You may use this, for instance,

- as a knowledge base to inform your customers about your products, services or procedures,
- for your employees to inform on internal business procedures,
- for your service staff to discuss procedures for helping customers, and much more.

You may reach the FAQ list at the **[FAQ]** menu. Click the icon on top of the list to enter a new FAQ. In Figure 3-32 you see the screen for a new FAQ entry. You may enter a question and an answer. In addition, you may

- link this entry to a product or service your company offers,
- assign a category for this entry,
- set a status for the entry.

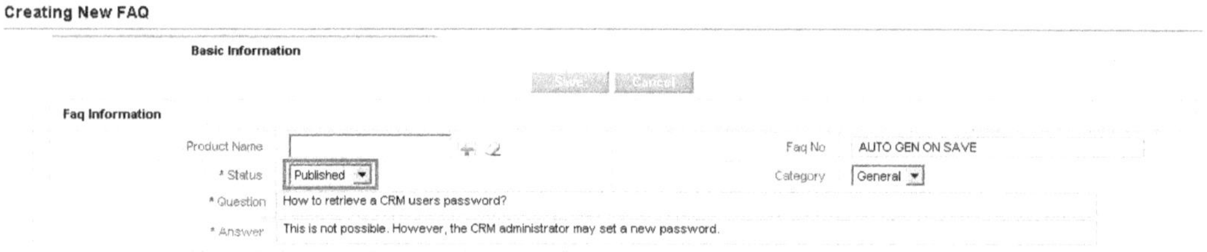

Figure 3-32: FAQ - Edit View

FAQ with the status **Published** will be visible at the Customer Portal.

3.2.4 Reporting and Analysis

The CRM provides you with several possibilities for evaluating your data according to criteria you have selected beforehand.

- **Dashboard:** The dashboard gives you a graphical representation of your sales and service data.

- **Reports:** You may summarize the data stored in the CRM using reports. There is a set of predefined reports available which you can customize to your needs. You should use these report and analysis features to get an overview of customer-related activities and to draw conclusions on how to improve your sales process.

3.2.4.1 Dashboard

The time period used at the dashboard does not automatically update with the passing time. You have to set the required period, and you should click **[Refresh] to** make sure the current data is shown.

You can reach the Dashboard function at the **[Dashboard]** menu. The dashboard includes a graphical representation of sales and services-related data as partly displayed in Figure 3-33.

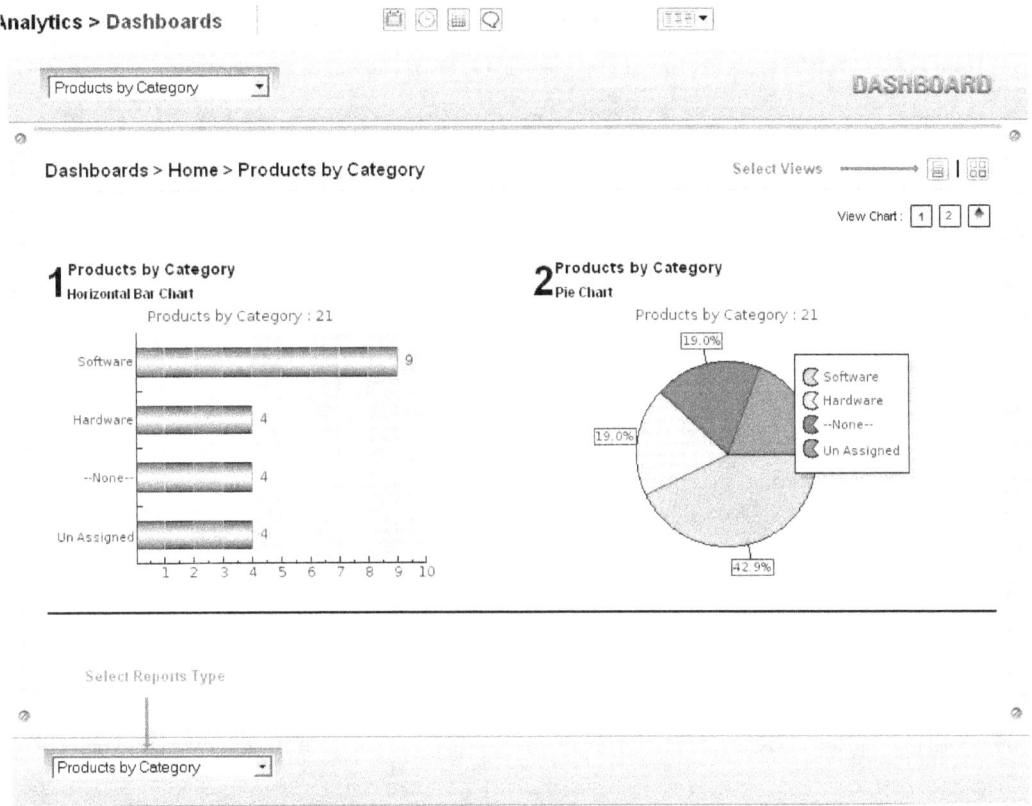

Figure 3-33: Dashboard

You may switch between different reports and views. Some reports, such as **Dashboard Home**, allow you to modify the period as well as the type of data included. Click **[Edit]** to modify the settings. Use the **CTRL button** on your keyboard to select multiple data sets to be displayed. The sales stages, status as well as the other source information used may get changed by your CRM system administrator.

3.2.4.2 Reports

You may get a report for almost any data you have stored in your CRM at the **[Reports]** menu as shown in Figure 3-34.

Figure 3-34: Reports Home

The CRM features a report generator as well as a report designer.

Report Generator:

The report generator offers reports which you can see on the screen or export as PDF or Excel files.

Report Designer:

The report designer allows you to select the data you want to see in a report and to modify its representation.

The CRM comes with a rich selection of standard reports as illustrated in the previous figure. Each of these reports comes as two types:

Tabular Report:

Tabular reports are the simplest and fastest way to get a listing of your data.

Summary Report:

Summary reports allow you to view your data along with subtotals and other summary information.

The following section explains how to modify reports or even set up your own report folders.

Edit Reports

To change existing reports click the **[Report Name]**. A new window will open which lists the selected report and allows customization.

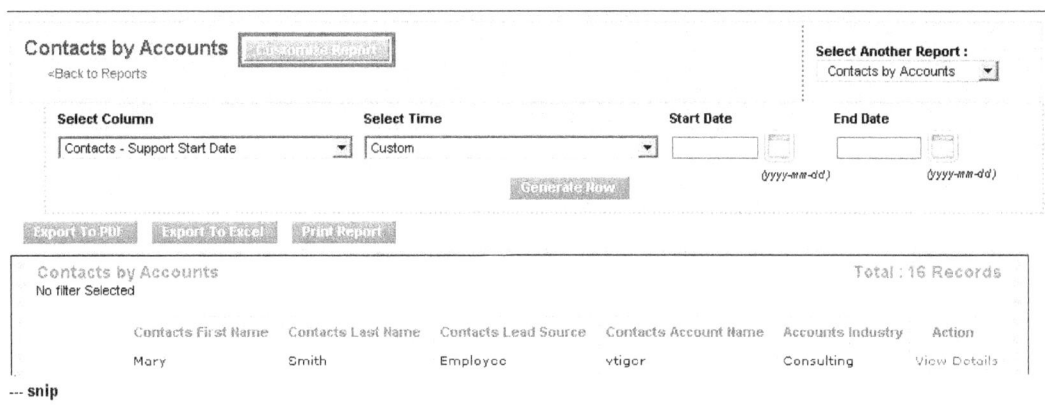

Figure 3-35: Report Detail View

To open the report editor to change an existing report, click **[Customize Report]** as indicated in Figure 3-35: Report Detail View. Follow the instructions.

To create a new report, click the **[New Reports]** icon shown in Figure 3-34: Reports Home. First you are asked for the CRM module which provides the data for the report. Based on this selection, the fields available for the reports are selected by the CRM system. The opening pop up window displays the next steps for report creation as shown in Figure 3-36: New Report - Detail View.

Figure 3-36: New Report - Detail View

Follow the instructions. Designing a report can be a very complex task. You should start with a very simple report and frequently check your results before beginning to use filter functions.

If your report design is finished, click **[Next]** to save your settings and to start the report generator. Then you

- can see the report at your screen,
- may export the report as PDF or Excel file, and
- may print the report.

Example: Let's assume you want to have a list of organizations who bought a specific product

You should follow these steps to create a report:

1. create a new report with a name, report folder and description
2. you will be asked for the related module; select Products
3. you will be asked for the format of the report; make your choice
4. select the fields you want have in the report
5. select the field in advanced filter as

    Product Name - equals - <name of your product>

Customized Report Folders

To create your own report folder, click the **[Create New Folder]** icon as shown in Figure 3-34: Reports Home. In the new pop up window, you may give this folder a name and a description. Click **[Save]** to create this folder. You could use this folder to store your own or modified reports. The new folder will be listed at the **[Reports]** menu. At this menu you may also move or delete reports by clicking the appropriate buttons or icons. You may create any report to be listed in your own folders. Select your folder in step 1 of the new report creation process.

3.2.5 Synchronizing CRM with Office Environment

The CRM comes with a set of programs which enhance the functionality of your office environment by linking your desktop computer with the CRM system.

Thunderbird Extension

The Thunderbird/Mozilla email client is an Open Source program that runs under Windows, Mac and Linux operating systems. It allows you to send and receive emails and contains an address book. You can think of it as a free version of Outlook. With the help of the Thunderbird Extension program you may:

- send emails you have received, to the CRM and store them in reference to the appropriate contact
- send contact information from your email client to the CRM
- receive contact information from your CRM

Please consult the Thunderbird extension manual for further information.

Outlook Plugin

Microsoft Outlook is very common in office environments. The Outlook plugin enhances the functionality of Outlook and allows users to synchronize data between Outlook and the CRM system. In detail you may:

- transfer any email to the CRM system and attach it to the appropriate contact
- synchronize your calendar
- synchronize your contacts
- synchronize your notes
- synchronize your tasks

Please consult the Outlook Plugin manual for further information. Note that there are additional and improved Outlook Plugin versions available as community contributions from vtiger's Extension site.

3.3 CRM User FAQ

The CRM support staff of crm-now maintains a CRM Journal which contains a frequently asked questions selection from CRM users not pertaining to a particular topic of this manual. You may find in the Journal answers to questions like:

Why is it important to distinguish between events and tasks?

How can I conveniently inform someone about a CRM entry?

Why should I use browser tabs in the list view?

Why should users not get administrator privileges?

How can I give the CRM's email signature a different look?

Why should I not delete Invoices?

and much more.

You may access the CRM Journal by the following URL: http://blog.crm-now.de/en/

4 Administrative Tasks

This chapter explains how the CRM system can be configured and managed by users with administrative privileges. It is very important that a CRM system administrator is capable of configuring the CRM according to the intended purpose and the company's business processes. Any skilled CRM administrator knows that understanding how things work is as important as knowing how things are done. Therefore, the following sections describe not only the CRM functions but also the basics of Role-based security and other business-related issues an administrator should consider.

4.1 Role-Based Security Basics

Role-based security has been implemented to control who is allowed to browse, delete or update information stored in the CRM. This section explains how to start working with the CRM's security settings and the role-based security concept as it is provided by the CRM system. It's an overview of all types of considerations an administrator should go through before starting to set up the CRM system.

4.1.1 Introduction to Role-Based Security

The CRM system operates on the basis of state-of-the-art security management which utilizes the concepts of roles, similar to the implementation of security in many current computer operating systems. Role-based security (also called Role-based access control) specifies and enforces enterprise-specific security policies in a way that maps naturally to an organization's structure. It has become the predominant model for advanced access control because it reduces the complexity and cost of security administration and is built on the premise that users are authenticated, which is the process of identifying the user. Once identified, roles and permissions are assigned to a user.

While Role-based security may be overkill in trivial settings (e.g. small enterprises with a couple of users who are all allowed to browse, delete or update all data) it is an extremely powerful tool for handling complex environments. This includes typical company settings where various sales teams or customer service teams need to browse, delete or update customer-related data while at the same time permissions on such data may vary depending on the function or task of an employee within the company. This concept is especially suited for companies:

- who want to have a larger number of people to work with the CRM simultaneously,
- who want to have restricted browse, delete or update capabilities for individual users, and
- who want to have an hierarchical privilege order implemented.

Although Role-based security does not promote any one protection policy, it has been shown to support several well-known security principles and policies that are important to commercial and governmental enterprises which process unclassified but sensitive information. These policies can be enforced when profiles are authorized for a role, when users are authorized as members of a role, at the time of role activation (e.g., when a role is established as part of a user's active session), or when a user attempts to perform an operation on data.

4.1.2 Definition of Terms

Definition of Users

There are two types of users for the CRM software:

- standard user
- administrator user

Standard users have limited access to the CRM system in order to perform CRUD (Create, Retrieve, Update, and Delete) and limited user-specific customization operations. Administrator users have unlimited privileges for the CRM. Administrator users are capable of managing the complete software including:

- managing users and groups and their access privileges,
- customizing the CRM user interface,
- creating communications templates,
- configuring all organization-wide settings,
- changing passwords, deactivating users, and viewing the login history and
- exercise CRUD operations for all data.

In figure: Special Admin Function you see the detail view of users provided by the CRM user management function. With marking the Admin check box any user will be assigned administration privileges and become an administrator user.

1. User Login & Role

User Name	standarduser	Admin	off
Password	Change Password	Email	
Status	Active	First Name	
Currency	Euro : €	Last Name	StandardUser
Default Lead View	Today	Role	Vice President
Default Calendar View	This Week		

------ snip   snip ------

Figure 4-1: Enable administrator access

At the core of role-based security stands the concept of collecting permissions in roles, which can be granted to standard users. Each role is based on one or more profiles. It is a user's membership in roles that determines the privileges the user is permitted to perform.

Security administration with role-based security consists of determining the operations that must be executed by persons in particular jobs, and assigning employees to the proper roles. The Role-based security framework provides for mutually exclusive roles as well as roles having overlapping responsibilities and privileges.

For example, some general CRM operations may be allowed for all employees, while other operations may be specific to a role. Role hierarchies are a natural way of organizing roles within an organization and defining the relationship and attributes of the roles. Complexities introduced by mutually exclusive roles or role hierarchies as well as regulating who can perform what actions, is all handled by the Role-based security settings.

For the CRM system to reach its full potential as a means for enterprise CRM, access control mechanisms must be in place which can regulate user access to information in a way that serves your business today.

Role-based security allows for the specification and enforcement of a variety of protection policies which can be tailored on an enterprise-by-enterprise basis. Once the Role-based security framework is established for the organization, the principal administrative actions are the granting and revoking of users into and out of roles as job assignments dictate.

One of the greatest advantages of Role-based security is the administrative capabilities it supports. User membership in roles can be assigned and revoked easily, and new memberships established as job assignments dictate. With Role-based security, users are not granted permission to perform operations on an individual basis, rather operations are associated with roles. Role association with new operations can be established as well as old operations deleted, as organizational functions change and evolve. This basic concept has the advantage of simplifying the understanding and management of privileges. Roles can be updated without having to directly update the privileges for every user on an individual basis.

Furthermore, individual users (e.g. John, Mary) might be assigned to one or more roles, where the roles are based on the user's job responsibilities and competencies in the organization. Users should be assigned to multiple roles to reflect the fact that some users connect to the system in different functions depending on the tasks. For example, user **John** might be assigned the role **Head-Sales**, because John is the head of sales at your company, as well as the role **admin**, because John is also CRM system administrator. If John wants to work as administrator he logs in as admin, if John wants to work as head of sales, he logs in as Head-Sales. It is possible to let John connect to the system with the same password, regardless of whether he acts as administrator or head of sales.

> Users in any given role can always view, edit and delete all data owned by users below in the hierarchy.

4.1.2.1 Definition of Profiles

Profiles are used to define privileges for executing CRM system operations. From a functional perspective, the central notion of role-based security is that of profiles representing actions associated with roles and users that are appropriately made members of roles.

The relationships between users, roles, and profiles are depicted in Figure 4-2: Users, Roles and Profiles Relations as many-to-many relationship. For example, a single standard user can be associated with one or more roles by different user names, and a single role can have one or more user members. Roles can be created for various job positions in an organization. For example, a role can include sales representatives or assistants in a company.

The profiles which are associated with roles, constrain members of the role to a specified set of actions. For example, within a sales organization the role of the sales representative can include operations to create, edit, and delete their own accounts; the role of an assistant can be limited to browse existing information of a particular sales rep, and the role of the head of sales may be to review all sales data.

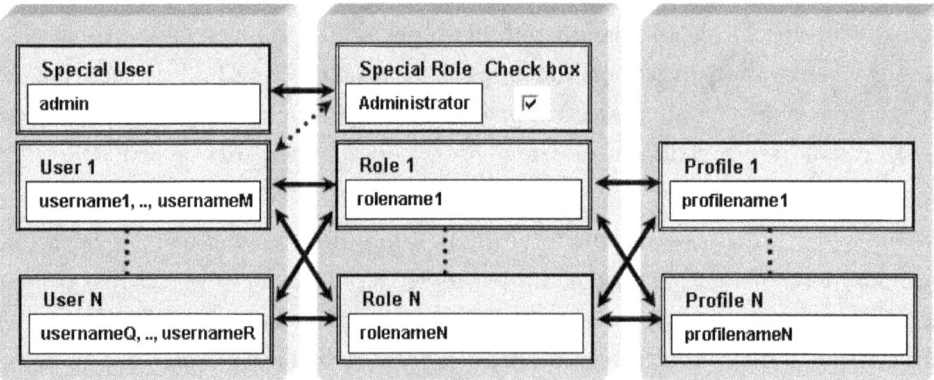

Figure 4-2: Users, Roles and Profiles Relations

The association of profiles with roles within an enterprise can be in compliance with rules that are self-imposed. Profiles can be specified in a manner that can be used in the demonstration and enforcement of regulations. For example, an assistant can be constrained to adding a new entry to a customer's history rather than being generally able to modify sales records.

Access privileges based on profiles are set by the CRM system administrator. The administrator has to set these privileges when configuring the CRM system. Therefore, the following privilege types are available:

- the permission to use certain CRM modules
- the permission to view data in certain CRM modules
- the permission to edit or to change data in certain CRM modules
- the permission to delete data in certain CRM modules
- the permission to export data from certain CRM modules
- the permission to import data to certain CRM modules

The CRM system makes sure that a user can only exercise certain operations if the user has proper privileges assigned.

> Note the following **General Rules**:
> - special privileges are always superior to common privileges
> - revoked privileges always override granted privileges
> - in addition, the CRM system maintains special rules in the following marked as **Important**

Table 4-1: Privilege Types

Privilege	Description
Global Privileges:	If you create a profile, the global privileges allow you to decide whether the common privilege to view or to edit all information / modules of the CRM system is given: • **View all:** A user with a role based on a profile that allows viewing all data, can view all data in the entire organization. You should not give this privilege if you want to implement restricted access rules. • **Edit all:** A user with a role based on a profile that allows editing all data, can edit all data in the entire organization. You should not give this privilege if you want to implement restricted access rules. **Important** Global privileges in profiles override the permissions defined by **Tab**, **Standard**, **Field** and **Utility Privileges** as they are explained below.
Tab Privileges:	The option to set tab privileges allows you to decide which tabs or modules should be shown. For this purpose the CRM displays all available modules. You may remove a menu tab by disabling all modules of a tab.
Field Privileges:	The option to set field privileges allows you to decide whether create, edit, delete, and view privileges are given for particular fields of a CRM module. For this purpose the profile menu displays all available fields, including custom fields.
Utilities	Numerous CRM modules come with utility functions such as import, export, merge and convert lead. The option to set utility privileges allows you to decide whether these functions will be available for roles that are based on a specific profile

> **Important**
>
> Privileges defined by profiles override the Default Organization Sharing Rules and the User defined Sharing Rules. For example, let us assume that the **organization sharing rule** allows a user to view the opportunities of others. However, if the profile does not allow access to the potential module these access privileges are revoked.

4.1.2.2 Definition of Groups

For better manageability, the CRM system allows collecting users, roles, roles with subordinates and user groups in groups. It is important to understand that groups are not a

> **Important**
>
> Group settings override the profile settings. Group privileges may become restricted by custom organization sharing privileges.

tool for defining security settings. Rather user groups are used to manage the data access.

Group of Users

The CRM system provides functions to define groups of users, sometimes called teams. You may give these groups their own name and assign an unlimited number of users to one group. As an example a group called Team A is shown in Figure 4-3: Group of Users - Example.

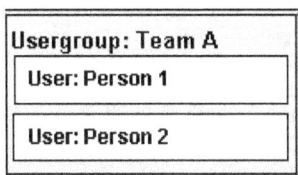

Figure 4-3: Group of Users - Example

Group of Roles

You can also build groups which are based on roles. That might be a helpful function if you do not know the individual users and their tasks within the company. An example is shown in Figure 4-4: Group of Roles - Example.

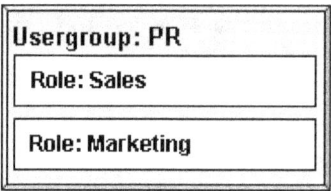

Figure 4-4: Group of Roles - Example

In this group all users that have the role Sales or Marketing are members of this group. If you assign a data entry at the CRM system to this group, all members become owners of this entry.

Group of Roles with Subordinates

In addition to simple Role-based groups you may also build groups which include subordinates. That means the users who are assigned to roles which are below a selected role will be included. The following figures illustrate this. Let's assume your company has set up a hierarchical order as shown in Figure 4-5: Roles - Hierarchy Example.

Figure 4-5: Roles - Hierarchy Example

In this figure the role "Sales" has a subordinated role "Sales Assistant" and the role "Marketing" is the master to the role "Marketing Assistant." If you create a user group as shown in Figure 4-6: Group of Roles with Subordinates - Example all users with sales and marketing-related roles, including the assistants will become members of this group.

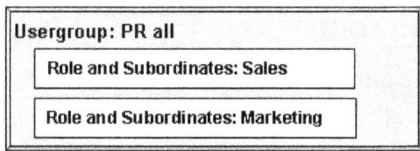

Figure 4-6: Group of Roles with Subordinates - Example

Group of Groups

You may build groups where the members are also groups. That means that all users who are a member of a selected group will also become members of the new group. Let's assume you want to build a hierarchy as shown in Figure 4-7: Sample Hierarchy for Groups. Based on this structure you may create a user group **Sales** where the groups **Team A** and **Team B** are members. At this example the **Team A** and **Team B** groups are built with users as members.

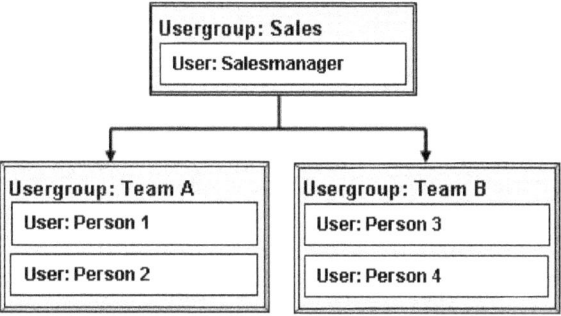

Figure 4-7: Sample Hierarchy for Groups

If you assign a CRM data entry to the group **Sales** the Persons 1 to 4 will all become the owners of this entry with all privileges.

4.2 CRM Administration

This section explains the administrative tasks required to manage the CRM system. It describes:

- the user administration and role-based security settings,
- the configuration of standard and custom entry fields,
- the templates and the configuration of other preset tools, and
- the basic system configuration.

For users with administration privileges the CRM system displays an additional **[Settings]** icon in the Navigation bar as shown in Figure 4-8. By clicking this icon a CRM configuration window will open which is only available to administrators.

It is advised that only one or a very limited number of users get administration privileges.

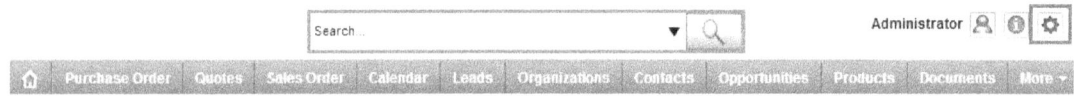

Figure 4-8: Additional Settings - Icon

4.2.1 User Administration

The user management functions are the core of the security management of the CRM system. They control the access to the CRM system based on the user's privileges. The following sections will explain in detail the purpose of these functions and the features available. You may look up the simple organization setup examples at the Appendix: Administration Examples or at the Appendix: Administration FAQ for further reference.

User Administration Basics

From the organization point of view, user administration means administration of privileges. Essentially, the use of privileges depends on the number of users and the company structure. Few users in small enterprises have few requirements for privilege administration. With an increasing number of users the complexity of the relations between the users increases and usually develops the need to assign and administer privileges.

The CRM system offers a privilege system that is based on the following simple looking rules:

- Who can see certain data?
- Who can change certain data?

- Who can delete certain data
- Who can create certain data?

In the CRM system, privilege **assignment primarily means the withdrawal of privileges**. In the practical work with the CRM this is most helpful and necessary as the following examples illustrate:

- A selling co-worker would certainly not be pleased, if somebody else changed the data of customers.
- Personal information remains confidential only if other co-workers are not allowed to see it.
- The company management does not want everybody to see the revenue figures.
- Only one person is allowed to change the product or service catalogue.

Therefore, it is necessary that the user privilege assignment is truly based on business requirements as described in the following examples:

- Only the sales staff is allowed to change customer related data.
- The secretary does not get any access to revenue numbers.
- Only the product manager is allowed to change prices of services or goods offered by the company.
- Only the management is allowed to see all CRM data.
- Nobody is allowed to export any contacts.

Considering the current CRM capabilities of managing user privileges you should configure your system in the following order:

Set the Default Organization Wide Privileges:

Organization Wide Privileges should be created first. They are the basis for the privilege assignment valid for all users.

Create Profiles:

Profiles are the basis for the privilege assignment to users. In any organization there are usually different users with different tasks, like sales, service, secretary or CRM administrator. Depending of the user type, the privileges for accessing data and using CRM modules and functions can be assigned.

Define Roles:

Roles are based on profiles and linked with the hierarchical order of the company. They define the overall privileges for each individual user.

Define Groups:

Larger organizations may define groups to improve the usability of the CRM system.

Create Users:

The privileges of individual users are defined by roles. You have to assign a role to a user.

Single users do not need any privilege management. They have and need all privileges to access and to change all data stored in the CRM. Nevertheless it is helpful to know the basics of privilege assignment. This might be needed if additional users will be needed in the future.

A small number of users, who use the CRM system together, should be familiar with the simple solutions offered by the privilege assignment. This includes particular:

- To prohibit that other CRM users see confidential data.
- To prohibit that other user can delete or modify data.

In a small organization there is usually no pronounced hierarchy between co-workers. A complex privilege administration does not have to be developed. However, if it should be necessary to granulate the privileges more finely, you should begin with the use of different profiles. Each individual user may get its own profile with certain privileges.

To provide a larger number of users within an organization with different user privileges, a clear structure of the privilege assignment is necessary. It is sensible to connect user privileges with the position or tasks of each individual user or user groups. The current CRM version supports a fine grained privilege management.

4.2.1.1 Users Configuration

To create or to manage users, click the **Users** menu to open the users list as shown in the following Figure 4-9: CRM Users - List View.

Never use a user login with administrator privileges for your daily work with CRM system.

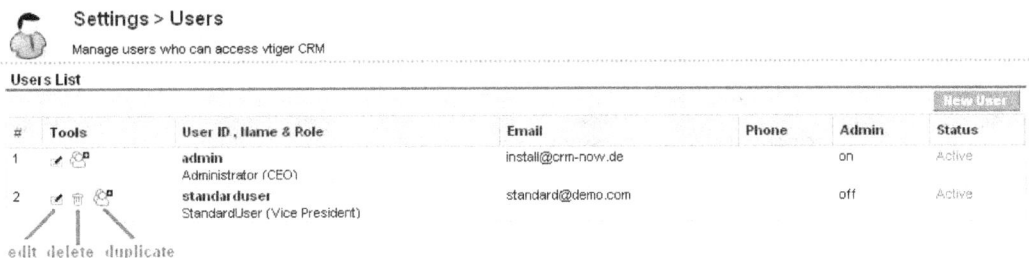

Figure 4-9: CRM Users - List View

This user list includes the user name, the role, the email address and other details for each individual active or inactive user. You may edit or delete users at this view.

If you want to delete a user click the 🗑 icon at a user's row. This function deletes a CRM user but not the user's data. You will be asked who you want to assign as the new owner of the data. You cannot delete the admin user.

Click the user's name (User ID) to open the detail view of a particular user as displayed at Figure 4-9. This view includes user master data related to the login and to the user's role and other user information. User information is not visible to other users. User privileges are not shown. These privileges are defined by the user profiles and organization-wide settings as it will be explained later.

Table 4-2: User Login & Role - Default entry fields

Entry Field	Description
User Name:	Each user must get a unique and secure user name. Use at least 8 digits. User names once created cannot be changed in the edit view.
Admin Checkbox:	Check this box only if you want to create a user with administrator privileges, independent from the role. It is suggested not to use that for normal operations.
Password:	Each user must get a unique and secure password. User name and passwords have to be a combination of small or capital letters and numbers. It is recommended that you use at least 8 digits. The more digits you have, the more secure is the CRM access. The use of special characters such as "-","/" or umlaut (such as ä, ö, ü or ß) as they are used in other languages as well as names with empty spaces or apostrophe are not allowed. Every user has the privilege to change the own password.

Entry Field	Description
First and Last Name:	Enter the user's name. The first name will be used for the welcome message. If you do not enter a first name, the last name will be used for the welcome message.
Role:	As explained before, roles define the privileges for a user. A role must be assigned to each individual user and must be created before.
Email:	Enter the email address of this user. This address will be used by the CRM for outgoing emails.
Status:	You may set a user as active or inactive. Inactive users are not allowed to login.
Default Activity View:	Here you can set the default activity view and decide how activities are presented to the user at the home page.
Default Lead View:	Here you can set the default lead view and decide how leads are presented to the user at the home page.
Currency:	You may set the currency for this user here. Note that the currencies available to the CRM system are defined by the currency settings menu.

Table 4-3: User Currency entries

Entry Block	Description
Currency:	You may set the currency for this user here. Note, that the currencies available to the CRM system are defined by the currency settings menu.
Digit Grouping Pattern:	Currency numbers can get grouped for display and PDF output. You may select your preferred grouping.
Digit Grouping Separator:	This sets the separator for the Grouping Pattern.
Decimal Separator:	This sets the decimal separator.
Symbol Placement:	You may decide whether you want to have the currency sign in front of the currency amount.

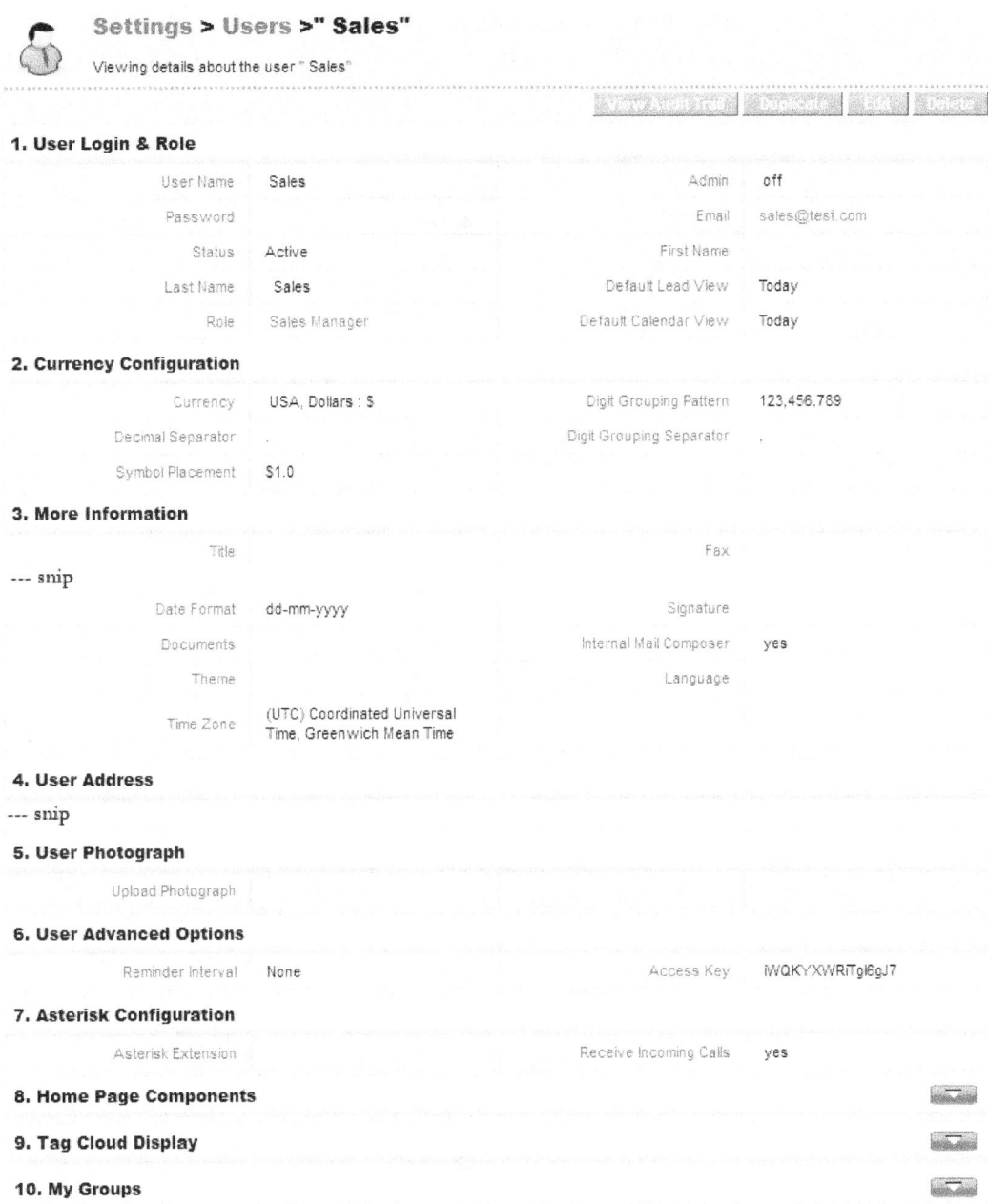

Figure 4-10: CRM Users - Detail View

Table 4-4: More Information - Default entry fields

Entry Field	Description
Reports to:	You may select the supervisor of the user. Note that this is only a reference and does not influence the security settings.

Signature:	You may enter an email signature. This signature will be added to every email which is send by the CRM automatically. You may use HTML tags give your signature a special format.
Internal Mail Composer:	This controls which mail program is used if you click on an email address. The default value is yes and this means that the CRM mail client is used. If you change it to no, the mail client installed on your computer is used for composing an email.

Table 4-5: Other User Settings Information

Entry Block	Description
3. Address Information	Enter the users address information.
4. User Image Information	You may store a photo of this user. Currently there is no further usage of such a photo in the CRM integrated.
5. User Advanced Options	You select the time interval on which your browser checks for activities stored at the CRM. A user will see a browser popup if an activity is due. The Access Key is provided by the CRM system for future use and can't get changed.
6. Asterisk Configuration	This setting is only valid, if the CRM communicates with an Asterisk PBX for incoming or outgoing phone calls. You enter your phone extension if applicable.
7. Home Page Components and 8. Tag Cloud Display	Each user may decide which CRM information will be collected at the users CRM Home page. Click Hide or Show to make your selection.
9. My Groups and 10. Login History	These entries are for information only. They cannot be edited. **My Groups** displays the group membership of a particular user. The **Login History** displays when a user has accessed the CRM system.

If you create a new user, note that an automatic email will be sent to this user with the login data. It is advisable to inform a prospect user in advance about the purpose of this email.

4.2.1.2 User Roles

The term Roles and their functions have been explained in the introduction section 4.1.

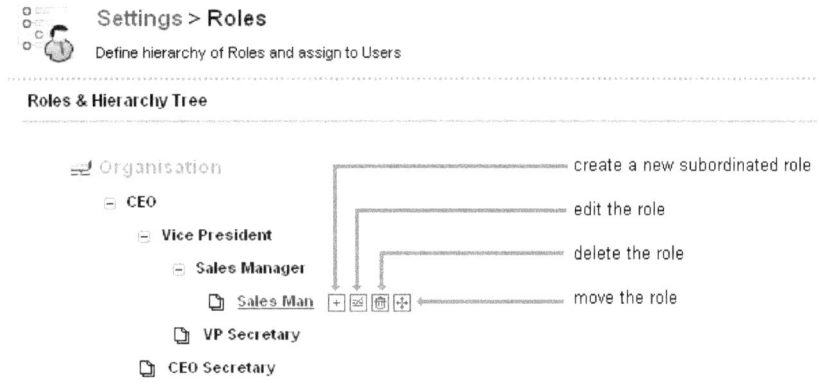

Figure 4-11: Roles - Company Hierarchy Example

Click the **Roles** menu to open the hierarchical role view as shown in Figure 4-11.

At this menu you are offered to add, edit, delete or move roles. Move your computer mouse pointer over a role entry. You will see a set of icons that allows you to perform these operations.

The "+" function creates a new role which is located in the hierarchical order one level below an existing role. Figure 4-12 displays a sample for an edit view of an existing or new role. You have to give the role a unique name and to decide which profiles will be associated with a particular role. Furthermore, the superior role will be displayed.

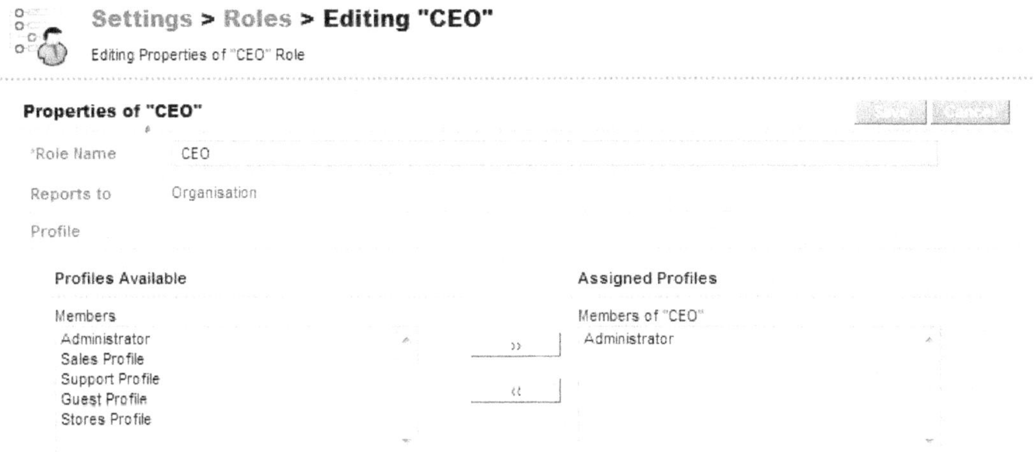

Figure 4-12: Role - Edit View

4.2.1.3 Profiles

All roles are based on profiles. With profiles you set the user privileges to access, change or delete data. The CRM system uses profiles in relation to the access privileges to modules and fields. Please note that the settings of the **Global Privileges** are always superior to the other privilege settings.

Click the **Profiles** menu to open the list view of your profiles as shown in Figure 4-13: Profiles - List View. Here you see a list of all profiles that have been defined in your CRM system. The CRM system comes with a set of pre-defined profiles which you can use and change but not delete.

Figure 4-13: Profiles - List View

Click the name of a profile to see the details. You may change a profile by clicking the **[Edit]** button. To create a new profile click the **[New Profile]** button at the list view. Follow the instructions provided:

Step One:

Give the profile a unique name and a description. Select whether you want to use an existing profile as a template. It is recommended to use this option. Click **[Next]** to continue.

Figure 4-14: New Profile - Step 1

Step Two:

The menu for step two is displayed in Figure 4-15: New Profile - Step 2. At this step you configure the access privileges for all modules. First you might select at the **Global Privileges** entry fields whether the profile allows to view or to edit all data.

Then you can configure the profile related access privileges for each individual CRM module. You may select Create/Edit, View and Delete privileges as well as the fields to be displayed in each module. Click **[Finish]** to save your profile at the CRM system.

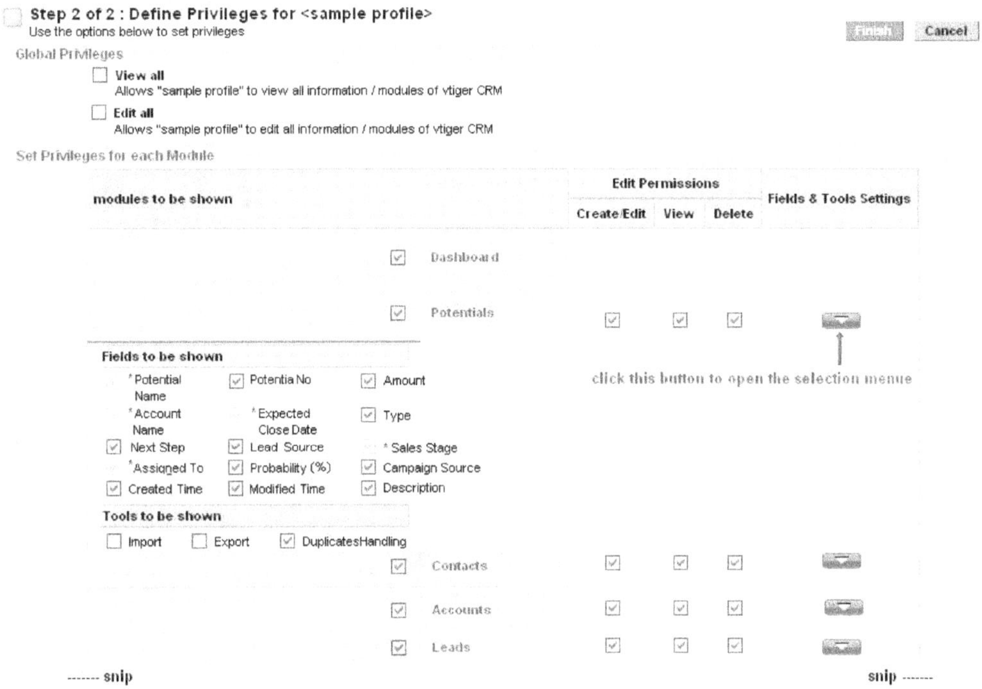

Figure 4-15: New Profile - Step 2

Note that a new profile always has a parent but can be edited independently. At the Appendix: Administration Examples you will find samples for profile configurations.

4.2.1.4 Groups

Groups are a very effective tool in order to summarize users and privileges. Any type of relationship can be used to form a group, such as:

- users at the same location
- users with a common task
- user at the same department
- users with the same working history
- users with the same interests

Click the **[Groups]** menu to open the list view as shown in Figure 4-16. You see a list of all existing groups.

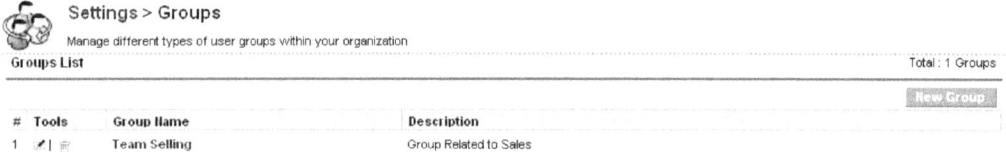

Figure 4-16: Groups - List View

Click the name of a group to get the details as shown exemplary in Figure 4-17. The detail view lists the name, the description and the current users who are members of this group. You may change the group settings by clicking the **[Edit]** button.

Figure 4-17: Groups - Detail View

To create a new group, click the **[Create New Group]** button at the list view. The new entry window as shown in Figure 4-18: Group - Create View allows you to define the conditions for a group.

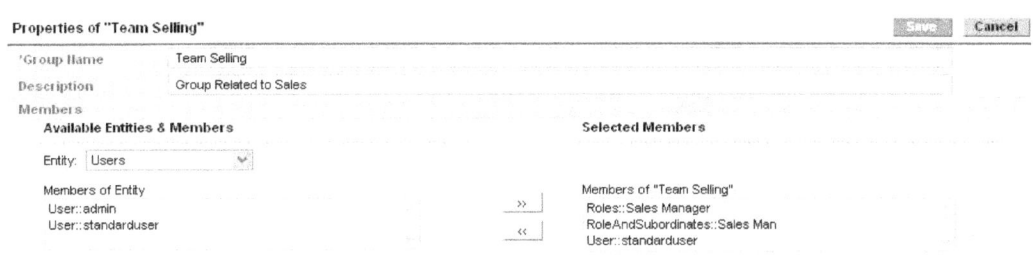

Figure 4-18: Group - Create View

To create a new group, click the **[Create New Group]** button at the list view. The new entry window as shown in Figure 4-18: Group - Create View allows you to define the conditions for a group.

First, give the group a name and provide a short description. Then select the criteria for a membership of this group. The filter function as well as the search function allows you to select members quickly. You may choose users, roles, roles and subordinates as well as other groups as group members.

Click **[Save]** to store your new group in the CRM system. The assignment of a user to a group will also be displayed at the users detail view as shown in Figure 4-10: CRM Users - Detail View.

4.2.1.5 Sharing Access

The CRM system allows you to set default privileges that are valid organization-wide. It is the purpose of this type of privilege to give an administrator tools that allow a fast overall security setting.

The **Sharing Access** privileges include **Global Access Privileges** and **Custom Access Privileges**. By default the sharing access settings allow all users to use all CRM features if not limited by profiles. In most cases there is no need to change this. However, if necessary you can restrict the access to individual modules within your organization.

Go to the **Sharing Access** menu to get an overview about the settings. The CRM system comes with default **Global Access Privileges** for the most important CRM modules as shown in Figure 4-19: Global Access Privileges - List View. These privileges control the data sharing at organization level.

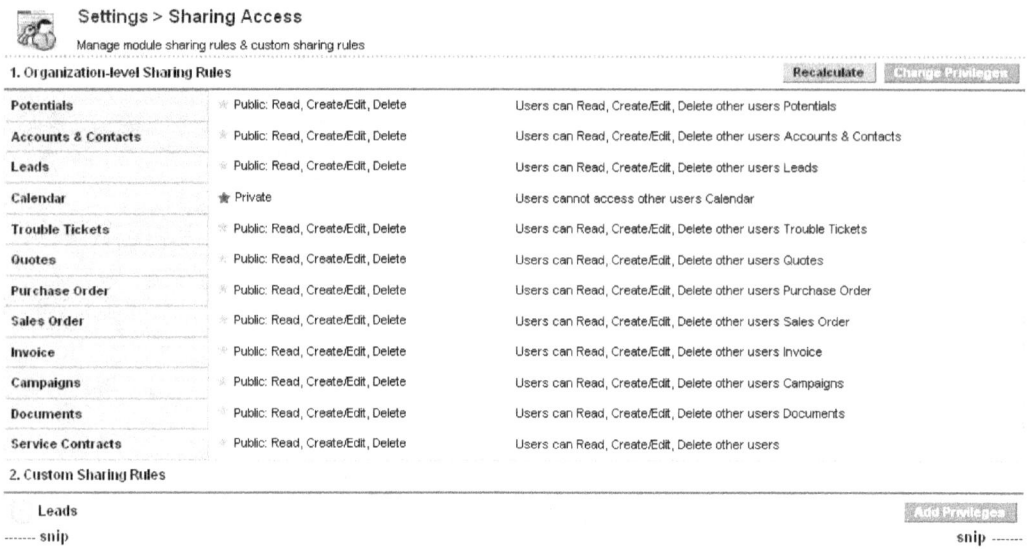

Figure 4-19: Global Access Privileges - List View

Profiles always override the organization wide sharing privileges! If you make changes to the sharing rules you must hit the **[Recalculate]** button to make your changes valid! Beware, based on the number of users and the sharing rules, the recalculate procedure may last a couple of minutes.

The following sharing permission types can be set:

Table 4-6: Sharing Permission Types

Type	Description
Private	Only the record owner, and users with a role which is above that of the record owner's role in the hierarchy, can browse, edit, delete and report on those records. That means by default a specific user can view only the data sets that are owned by the user, owned by a group where the user is a member, owned by subordinate users, or shared to the user.
Public Read Only	All users can view and report on records but not edit them. Only the owner, and users with a role which is above that of the record owner's role in the hierarchy, can edit or delete those records.

Type	Description
Public Read/Write	All users can view, edit all records. Only the owner, and users with a role which is above that of the record owners role in the hierarchy, can delete those records.
Public	All users can view, edit and delete all records.

Please note the following rules:

- Default organization sharing privileges are overridden by profile settings.
- For the activities module the default organization sharing privilege value is set to the fixed value **Private** and cannot be altered.
- Regardless of the organization-wide defaults, users can always view and edit all data owned by or shared with users below them in the role hierarchy if not prohibited by the profile.
- When an organization access has been set to **Private**, the access to related opportunities, tickets, quotes, sales orders, purchase orders, and invoices is also set to private. You must have at least read access to a record to be able to add activities or other associated records to it.

This menu cannot be used for controlling calendar access privileges. You may configure the sharing access at the calendar settings menu as described in section *2.2.1 Calendar*.

In addition, you may create user defined sharing rules set by **Custom Sharing Rules**. These functions allow the administrators to selectively grant data access to a set of users. Custom data sharing rules can be created to share module related data between the following entities:

- From Role to Role
- From Role to Role with Subordinates
- From Role to Group
- From Role with Subordinates to Role
- From Role with Subordinates to Role with Subordinates
- From Role with Subordinates to Groups

- From Group to Role
- From Group to Role with Subordinates
- From Group to Group

Sharing Rules can be created for the following modules:

Table 4-7: Sharing Rules for Modules

Module	Description
Leads:	Leads owned by the users of a given Role/Role Subordinates/Group can be shared with users of another Role/Role Subordinates/Group with Read Only or Read/Write permission. Emails related to a lead will also be shared with Read Only or Read/Write permission.
Organizations:	Organizations owned by the users of a given Role/Role Subordinates/Group can be shared with users of a Role/Role Subordinates/Group with Read Only or Read/Write permission. Emails related to an organization will also be shared with Read Only or Read/Write permission.
Opportunities:	Opportunities owned by the users of a given Role/Role Subordinates/Group can be shared with users of a Role/Role Subordinates/Group with Read Only or Read/Write permission. Quotes and Sales Order related to an opportunity will also be shared with Read Only or Read/Write permission.
Trouble Tickets:	Tickets owned by the users of a given Role/Role Subordinates/Group can be shared with users of a Role/Role Subordinates/Group with Read Only or Read/Write permission.
Email:	Emails owned by the users of a given Role/Role Subordinates/Group can be shared with users of a Role/Role Subordinates/Group with Read Only or Read/Write permission.
Quotes:	Quotes owned by the users of a given Role/Role Subordinates/Group can be shared with users of a Role/Role Subordinates/Group with Read Only or Read/Write permission. Sales Orders related to a quote will also be shared with Read Only or Read/Write permission.
Purchase Order:	Purchase Orders owned by the users of a given Role/Role Subordinates/Group can be shared with users of a Role/Role Subordinates/ Group with Read Only or Read/Write permission.

Module	Description
Sales Order:	Sales Order owned by the users of a given Role/Role Subordinates/ Group can be shared with users of a Role/Role Subordinates/Group with Read Only or Read/Write permission. Invoices related to a sales order will also be shared with Read Only or Read/Write permission.
Invoice:	Invoices owned by the users of a given Role/Role Subordinates/Group can be shared with users of a Role/Role Subordinates/Group with Read Only or Read/Write permission.

Sharing Rules created for the Organizations module will automatically apply to the Contacts module. Please note the following general sharing rules:

- Custom Sharing Rules can only extend the visibility, but they cannot hide it.
- Sharing Rules cannot be specified to share data between two users. (If you want to do this, please refer to Appendix: Example II.)
- Sharing rules apply to all existing data and the data which will be added in future.
- The number of sharing rules which can be defined for a single Role, Role Subordinates or Group is not limited.

4.2.1.6 Fields Access

The function available at the default organization Field Access menu is used to control the visibility of fields in various modules for the entire organization. You can use this function to either show or hide entry fields to the entire organization. Default field access settings include custom fields you may have created before. By default the CRM is configured as to display all master data which are provided in the CRM system. As an example, in Figure 4-20: Fields Manager for Calendar, you see the default fields for the FAQ. If you want to restrict access to specific fields, you can edit and change the settings for each individual CRM module.

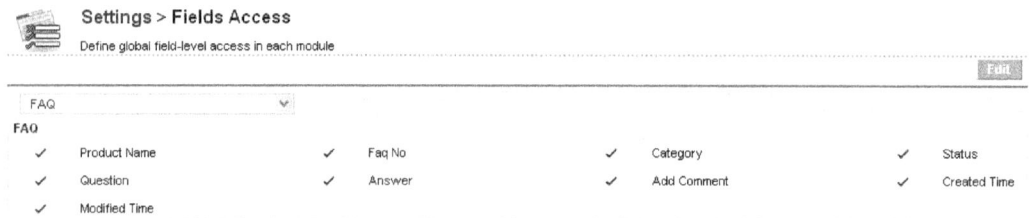

Figure 4-20: Fields Manager for Calendar

Important:

- It is not possible to disable the mandatory fields in the modules.
- Default Organization field access overrides the profile level field access.

For example, let us assume a profile allows viewing the website field in leads. However, if this field has not been enabled at the organization level field access settings it will not be displayed.

4.2.1.7 Audit Trails

You may want to know what a particular user has been done in the CRM system. For this type of audit open the **Audit Trail Information** menu as shown in the next figure.

Figure 4-21: Audit Trail - Configuration Menu

To configure an audit trail for a particular user, select a user name at the drop down menu and mark the check box. Immediately you will see a display message that indicates that the audit trail has been enabled.

Audit Trails			
Showing 1 -3 of 3			
Module	Action	Record ID	Action Date
Calendar	CalendarAjax		2009-02-05 17:52:36
Accounts	EditView	8	2009-02-05 17:52:34
Accounts	AccountsAjax		2009-02-05 17:52:32

Figure 4-22: Audit Trail - Report

To see the collected data, select the user's name and click the **[View Audit Trail]** button. A new window will open which displays the collected data, as shown in Figure 4-22: Audit Trail - Report. You may stop an audit trail by removing the check box mark for a particular user. Immediately you will see a display message that indicates that the audit trail has been disabled. Note that the audit trail function might slow down the CRM system.

4.2.1.8 User Login History

As CRM system administrator you may want to know who has accessed the system. At this menu you may get the login history for each individual user. Open the menu and select a user then you will see the login details, as illustrated in Figure 4-23: User Login History. Note, that the login date and time are always displayed.

The logout data are only available if a user used the logout button.

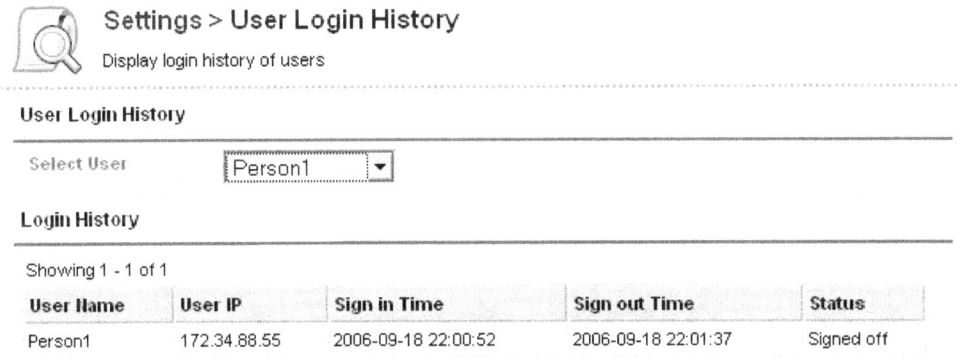

Figure 4-23: User Login History

4.2.2 Studio

The studio allows you to customize your master data, to modify the content of the pick lists in each individual module and to add or remove CRM modules as explained in the following sections.

4.2.2.1 Module Manager

The Module Manager allows you to add new CRM modules to the CRM and to configure the content and the display structure of your existing modules.

Installation of new CRM modules

With Module Manager, installation of CRM addons can be accomplished with a few simple clicks. Such addons can enhance the CRM's functionality substantially.

The vtiger community is providing such enhancements on its extension web site at https://www.vtiger.com/add-ons/. To find an extension which is compatible to your CRM version and supported by the Module Manager, look for the compatibility information.

To install an extension look for the install instructions provided with the extension module. The standard procedure is as follows:

- Download the extension. The standard file format is <module name>.zip. Do not unzip this file.
- Goto [Settings] -> [Module Manager] -> [Custom Modules] as shown in the following figure and click the [Import New] button.

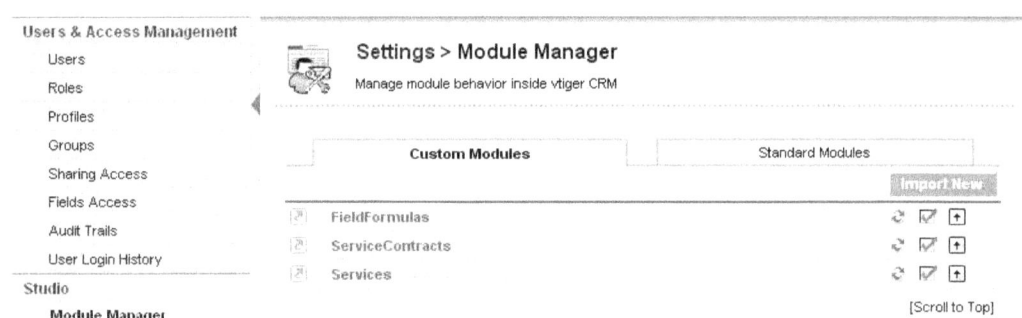

Figure 4-24: Installing New CRM Module

- Follow the instructions to upload the extension to your CRM. During the update the CRM verifies the file structure and compatibility of the extension and reports possible problems. In any case it is recommended to make a backup of your existing CRM before you install any extension.

CRM Layout Editor

The layout editor allows adding and deleting custom fields, moving fields within a view, set and remove mandatory field, rearranging fields as well as related lists as displayed at the **More Information** tab of modules.

To access the editor click the **[Standard Modules]** tab. You will see a list of all modules as illustrated in Figure 4-25. At this view you may enable or disable individual CRM modules for all CRM users or access the layout editor.

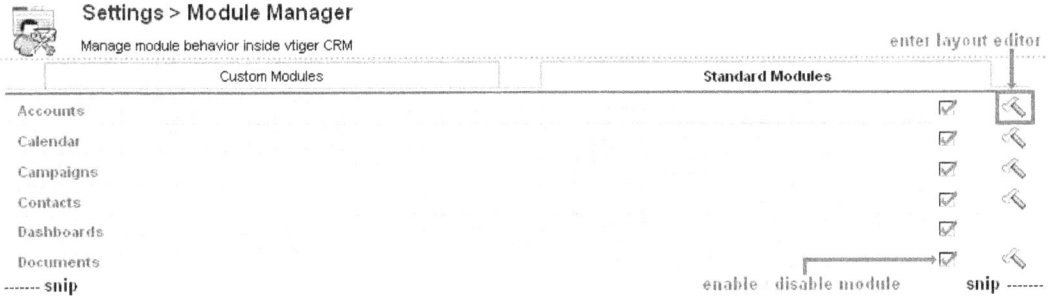

Figure 4-25: Module Manager - Standard Modules

At the CRM all information displayed are organized in so-called blocks. Each block represents an information unit. The purpose and the content of blocks are configurable. You may create additional blocks if needed. The block structure and related functions are illustrated in the following figure.

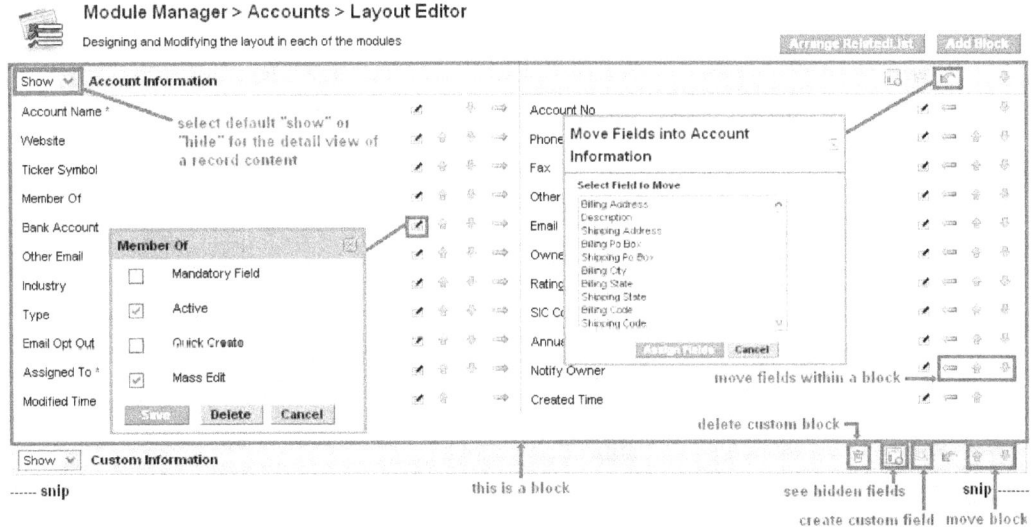

Figure 4-26: Layout Editor

The following table summarizes the available functions.

Table 4-8: Layout Editor Functions

Function Type	Function	Description
Block Functions	add and delete blocks	You may add a new custom block by clicking the Add Block button. You have to give this block a unique name. You may delete custom blocks only.
	see hidden fields in blocks	As displayed in the following figure you may set a fields "member of" property as Active or Inactive (check box unchecked). If inactive, the field will not be displayed. If you want to see a list of the inactive fields click on the appropriate icon.
	move blocks	You may change the order on which the blocks are displayed in a detail view by clicking the appropriate icons.
	show and hide blocks	The show and hide function sets the default detail view for a block. If hided the blocks head line is still displayed and can get expanded to a full view if needed.
Field Functions	create a field	You may create a new custom field by clicking on the appropriate icon. In section: Custom Fields the process of field creations is explained in detail.
	active and inactive fields	Click on the appropriate icon to see the "member of" property of a field. You may set a field as active or inactive. Inactive fields will not get displayed.
	delete a field	You may delete custom fields only at the "member of" property menu by clicking the **[Delete]** button. This button is not provided for CRM standard fields which cannot get deleted. Instead, hide such standard fields if not needed.
	move fields within blocks	You may change the order on which the block fields are displayed in a detail view by clicking the appropriate icons.

Function Type	Function	Description
	move fields between blocks	You may move a field into a block by clicking the appropriate icon. You will get a list of fields which can get moved. By clicking the [Assign Fields] button you move the field from one block to the destination
Control more Information Tab Order	arrange related lists	Each detail view has related modules which you can see if you hit the More Information tab in a detail view. You may change the display order of this information by clicking the [Arrange Related List] button.

Custom Fields

You may configure your own entry fields for most of the CRM modules as explained in the previous section. By clicking the appropriate icon a new window will open as displayed in Figure 4-27: Custom Field Definition.

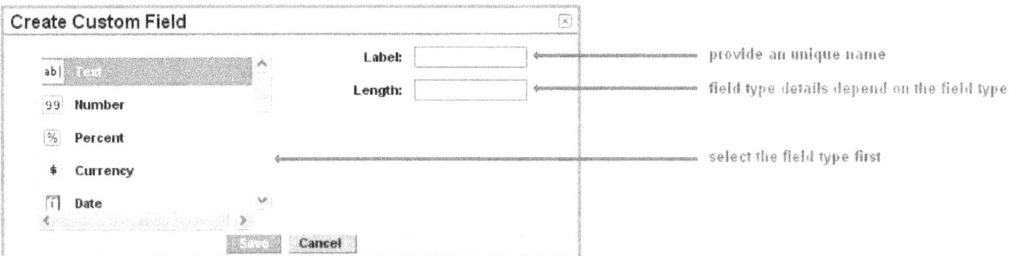

Figure 4-27: Custom Field Definition

In order to create a new field you have to select the data format first. The following table lists the available formats. Make sure that each custom field gets a unique name as label.

Table 4-9: Custom Field Definitions

Field Type	Content
Text	[Length:] Enter the maximum number of characters, e.g. 10 for ten characters.
Number	[Length:] Enter the maximum number of digits, e.g. 10 for ten digits; [Decimal Places]: Enter the number of decimal places you want to have, e.g. 0 has no decimal places, 1 creates one decimal place, like 55.4 and so on.
Percent	[Length:] Enter the maximum number of digits, e.g. 3 for three digits; [Decimal Places]: Enter the number of decimal places you want to have, e.g. 0 has no decimal places, 1 creates one decimal place, like 55.4 and so on.

Field Type	Content
Currency	[Length:] Enter the maximum number of digits, e.g. 6 for six digits; [Decimal Places]: Enter the number of decimal places you want to have, e.g. 0 has no decimal places, 1 creates one decimal place, like 55.4 and so on.
Date	Just give the field a name.
Email	Just give the field a name.
Phone	Just give the field a name.
Pick List	You may create this pick list by using a new line for each entry.
URL	Just give the field a name.
Check Box	Here you may define a check box (yes/no). Just give the field a name.
Text Area	This is a field where you may enter up to 255 characters of text.
Multi-Select Combo Box	You may create a list by using a new line for each entry. In contrast to the Pick List you will be able to select multiple entries at once.
Skype	You may use this custom field to link the CRM System with the Skype application running at your client computer. Just give this field a unique name. At your edit view of the related CRM module you may enter a Skype ID or a phone number. For more information about Skype look at http://www.skype.com.

Make a note of the field name and properties you created. You will need this when you want to create references to a custom field.

Custom fields for leads are special. You may decide what will be done with the content stored in these fields when you convert a lead to a sales opportunity. You may drop this information or transfer the content of these fields to corresponding custom fields at opportunities, organizations or contacts.

You should adopt the following procedure to prepare the transfer of custom fields from leads for further use:

1. Create custom fields for opportunities, organizations or contacts in reference to custom fields in leads. E.g., if you have created a custom field with the name **bank account** for leads, you should create custom fields for opportunities, called **account No**. It is recommended not to use the same name.

2. Open the **Leads Custom Field Mapping** module (only displayed for leads) at **[Studio]>[Module Manager]>[Standard Modules]** after clicking the **Layout Editor** icon for leads.

3. A new window will open as shown in Figure 4-28: Map Lead Custom Fields.

4. All custom fields created for leads are displayed. Select the mapping to the corresponding fields in contacts, organizations or opportunities you want to have. In the figure's sample, you see that the Contact custom field **Bank Account No** has been assigned to the **Bank Account** field of Leads.

5. Click [**Save**] to transfer your settings to the CRM system.

When finished the mapped custom fields are linked and will be used when you convert a lead into an opportunity as described in section *3.2.2 Working with Opportunities*.

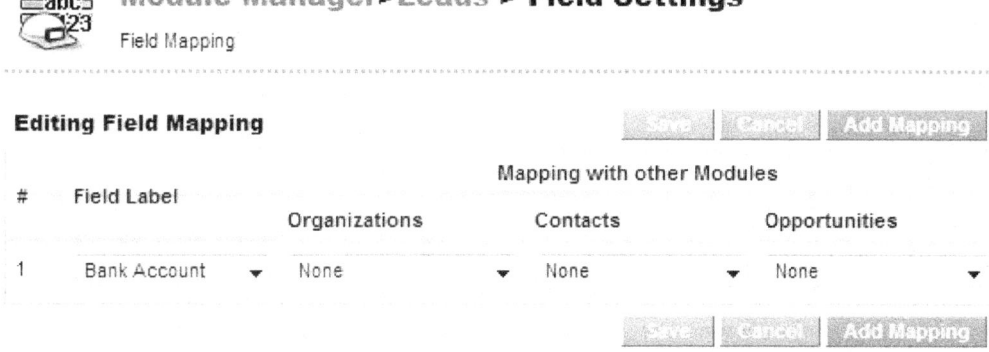

Figure 4-28: Map Lead Custom Fields

The format and the type of the custom fields in leads and the corresponding custom fields in opportunities, organizations, or contacts must be absolutely identical!

Tool Tip Management

The tool tip management feature provides mouse over functions to certain fields in list views. This allows you to see selected parts of a record content without open it. Figure 4-29 illustrates a sample for a FAQ entry.

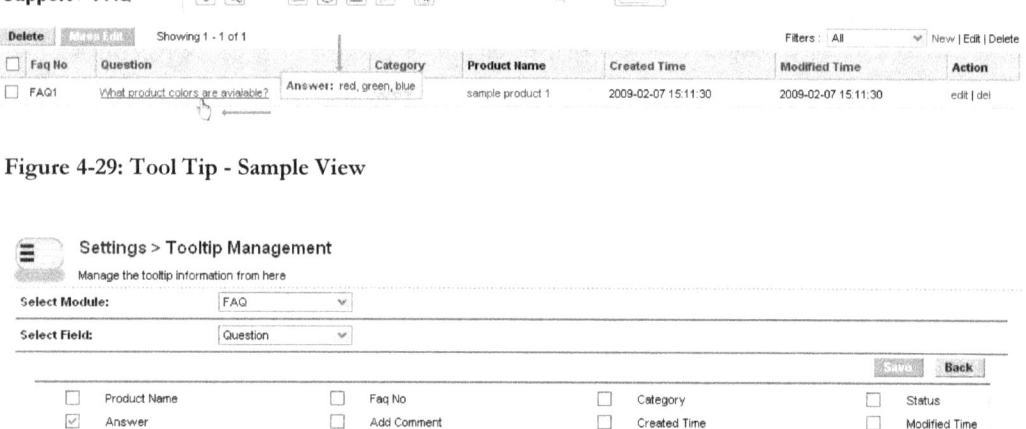

Figure 4-29: Tool Tip - Sample View

Figure 4-30: Tool Tip - FAQ Menu

To achieve the view as shown in the sample you need to open the **[Tool Tip Management]** menu. Select the module and the field to which you would like to have a mouse over popup displayed. Add the fields from which you want to see the contents by marking the appropriate check boxes. Save your settings. An example that relates to the previous figure is shown in Figure 4-30.

Field Formulas

At the Module Manager you may add custom fields with a content which is generated automatically by a calculation based on other existing fields. The following illustrates how you can setup such an equation for an Opportunity field. You may follow the same steps for other modules for which this function is available.

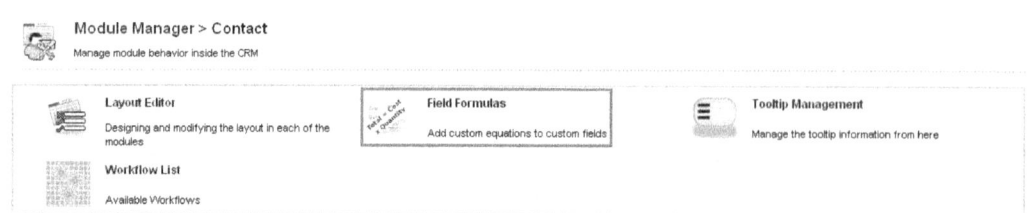

Figure 4-31: Field Formulas in Module Manager

Before you can setup any equation you need to create a custom field with a string or the integer number format for your particular module. When done go to the Module Manager and select the module and click the appropriate icon as displayed in Figure 4-31.

The formula list view opens. By clicking the **[New Field Expression]** button (which is only available if a custom field has been created), the edit view opens as shown in Figure 4-32. In this menu you may create your equation.

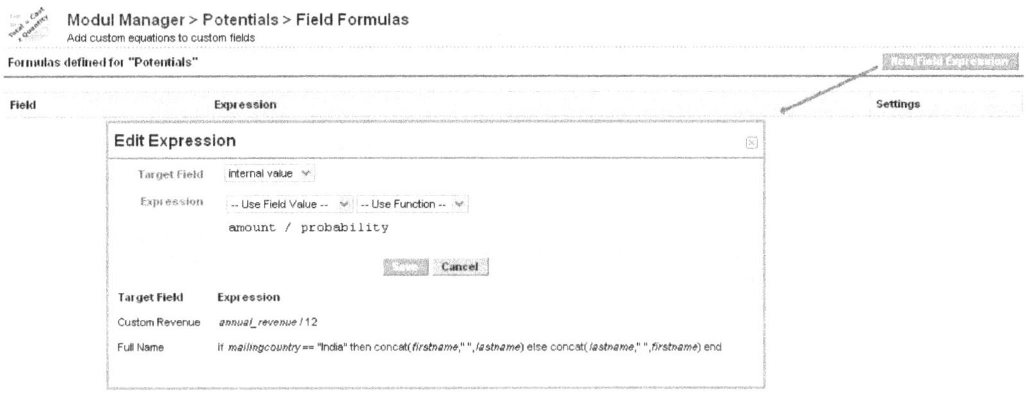

Figure 4-32: Field Formulas - Edit View

Currently there are two types of equations possible:

- **String Operations**: You may combine strings to a new string based on certain criteria. The CRM provides the **Concact Function** for your operation which returns concatenated strings. You may combine it with conditions as shown in the following example.

> If mailingcounty = "USA" then **concat** lastname "," ,firstname else **concat** lastname " ",firstname

The concat function is a direct data base operation and will return Null if one of the values is not defined.

For more detailed information please refer to a data base manual, available for instance at http://dev.mysql.com/doc/refman/5.0/en/string-functions.html.

- **Mathematical Operations**: You may combine numbers to a new number by using mathematical functions. These functions can be any basic arithmetic operation but also some logical operations supported by the data base. The following is a simple example:

  In reference to the settings in Figure 4-32: Field Formulas - Edit View this operation will fill the custom field **internal value** with a value which is the result of dividing the

  $$\text{amount / probability}$$

  Amount of the Opportunity by the Probability. Please refer to the data base manual for further options.

After you have setup an equation, the custom field of the particular module will get its values from the defined formulas whenever an entry is saved.

4.2.2.2 Picklist Editor

Picklists are drop down menus which are offered to you at the Edit or Ajax View of several CRM modules. This menu allows you to define the content of the pick lists based on the roles.

Click the **[Picklist Editor]** menu to get an overview about the CRM modules which have pick lists included, as shown in Figure 4-33. You have to select a module first to see the available picklists.

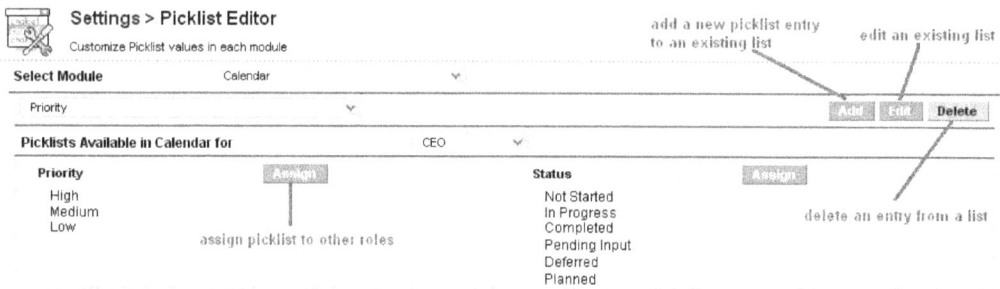

Figure 4-33: Studio - Picklist Editor

All pick lists are roles related. That means that the content of the pick list for each individual (non admin) user depends on the role which has been assigned to this user.

You may use this feature for instance to create pick lists in different languages or to restrict the users access to certain entries. Click the **[Assign]** button to select the roles to which a displayed picklist applies.

To modify the pick list content, select a CRM module first and choose a corresponding picklist as well as the role. The display of the available pick lists will change accordingly. To change the content of a pick list use the buttons as explained in the figure. At the new window which pops up you may make your changes.

Click **[Save]** to transfer your changes to the CRM system.

> Some content of the pick lists cannot be changed. This content is defined by the system settings. Please contact your CRM system provider if content is provided which does not fit to your needs.

4.2.2.3 Picklist Dependency Setup

Existing Picklists, or Picklists which had been created by the Module Manager, can be used to a select a single or multiple entries only. The Picklist Dependency Setup menu allows you to link contents of a Picklist with content of another Picklist. That means, that you may control the content of a Picklist displayed in the menu by the selected content of another Picklist.

The following description uses a sample to explain the functionality. Let us assume we have added two Picklists to the menu as shown in the following Table 4-10.

Table 4-10: Dependency Picklist Sample

Picklist 1		Picklist 2	
Name	Content	Name	Content
Product type	--None--	Products	--None--
	Fruits		Potatoes
	Vegetables		Cabbage
	Others		Peas
			Apples
			Plum
			Pears
			Packing Crates

We would like to control the content of Picklist 2 and display in Picklist 2 only content which relates to Picklist 1. For instance, if we select Vegetables in Picklist 1 we would like to see only Potatoes, Cabbage and Peas in Picklist 2.

Open the **Picklist Dependency Setup** menu as shown in the Figure 4-34.

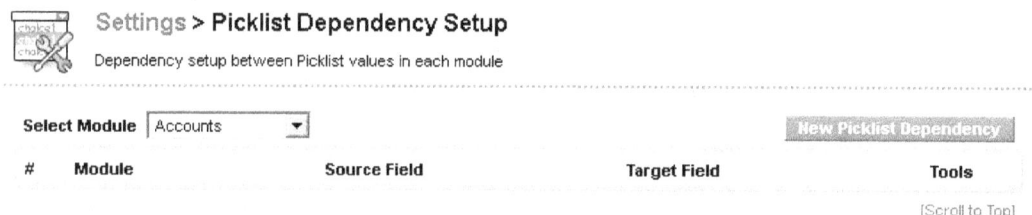

Figure 4-34: Picklist Dependency - List View

Select the module Organizations and click the button **[New Picklist Dependency]** to reach the Create View as shown in Figure 4-34.

Figure 4-35: Picklist Dependency - Create View

You use this menu to define the dependencies. The **Target Field** gets controlled by the **Source Field**. Select the appropriate Picklists for both fields as shown in the figure.

Click **[Next]** to define the concatenation of the Picklist content. The follow up menu, as shown in Figure 4-36, provides you the option to set Picklist fields in relations to each other.

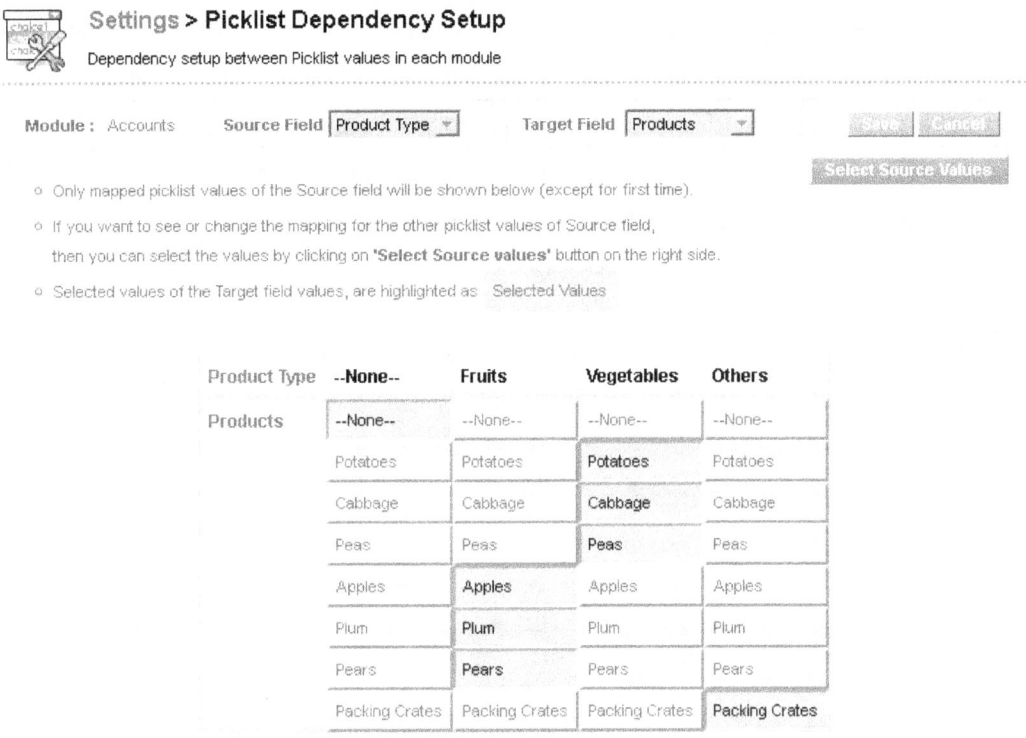

Figure 4-36: Picklist Dependency - Concatenation Menu

The column heading contains the content of Picklist 1. It is recommended that you unselect column by column the fields you do not want to see in Picklist 2 as shown in this example.

The button **[Select Source Values]** allows you to exclude columns from the mapping.

You may use one Source Field to control the content of multiple Target Fields.

4.2.2.4 Menu Editor

You may configure the Navigation Area of your CRM and create a menu order which fits better to your companies' needs. When you open the **[Menu Editor]** menu, you see at the left side a list of all available and active CRM modules, as illustrated at Figure 4-37.

At the right side you see a list of selected module. Be aware of the order. The first 10 entries are displayed at the Navigation Area directly. Beginning with the 11th entry in this list, the menu items are getting displayed at the **More** menu.

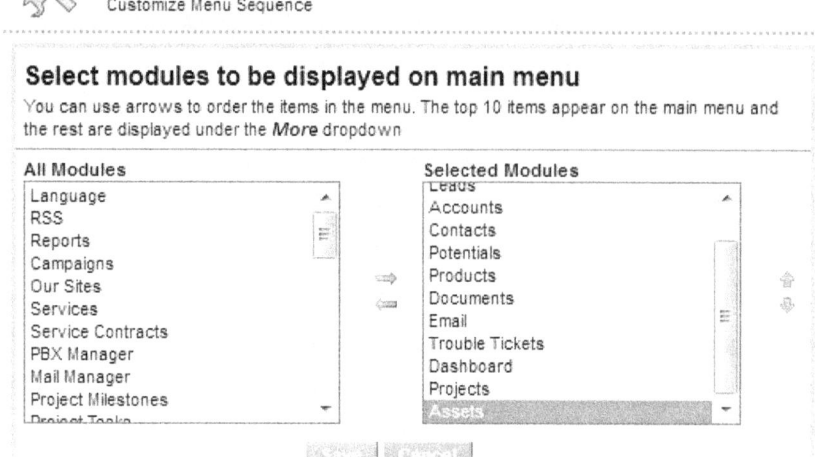

Figure 4-37: Menu Editor - Edit View

You may sort the order on the left side by clicking the blue arrows. You may add or remove a menu by clicking the green arrows. You may not remove the **Home** and the **More** menu. Click **[Save]** to activate your selection.

4.2.3 Communication Templates

Communication templates intend to help you to work with the CRM more efficiently. The CRM allows you to create and to use templates for a wide variety of purposes. The following sections explain the details.

4.2.3.1 Notification Scheduler

The CRM may automatically send notifications on special events by emails. Click the **[Notification Schedulers]** menu to see the status of the notification scheduler and all message types as shown in Figure 4-38.

Settings > Notification Schedulers
Manage Notifications that will alert in case of important actions

Notification Schedulers

#	Notification	Description	Status	Tool
1	Delayed Task Notification	Notify when a task is delayed beyond 24 hrs	Active	
2	Big Deal Notification	Notify on completion of big deal	Active	
3	Pending Tickets Notification	Notify for getting attention to status of tickets which are pending	Active	

------ snip   snip ------

Figure 4-38: Notification Schedulers - List View

Use the **[Tool]** icon to activate or to deactivate a notification and to determine the content of a notification.

All active notifications will be sent as emails if the conditions are met. They will be sent to the owner of a particular contact, opportunity or ticket. The messages about the upcoming end of a support case will be send to the owner of the module as explained in Section 4.2.4 part *Assign Module Owners*.

> At the current release the CRM administrator cannot modify the causes for notifications. The big deal notification is set to the value of 10.000 of your currency. You should contact your software provider if you want to have this changed. This provider may also help you to configure the threshold values for Delayed Tasks and Pending Tickets. The messages for too many tickets are related to a particular organization, and Support Starting & Ending dates to customers.

4.2.3.2 Inventory Notifications

You may use the CRM system for automatic notifications to the inventory manager if certain conditions occur. Click the **Inventory Notification** menu or look at the following figure for a description of these conditions. Note that you can assign the product handler for individual goods or services at the product catalogue as described in section 2.5 Product - Related Entries. You can determine which messages will be sent to the buying agent of your company. Click the **[Tools]** icon related to a notification to make modifications.

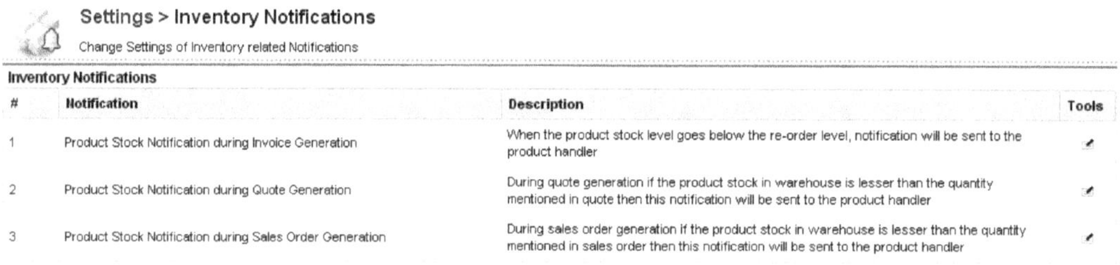

Figure 4-39: Inventory Notifications

4.2.3.3 Email Templates

If you use the CRM for sending standard emails frequently it is most helpful to have such emails available as templates. To see any existing email template list, click the **[Email Templates]** menu.

The CRM comes with templates as listed in Figure 4-40. You may modify existing templates or create an unlimited number of new templates. Note, that there are public and private templates. Public templates are available to all CRM users. Private templates are only provided to particular users.

Figure 4-40: Email Templates - List View

Click the templates name to see the detail view of an existing template. An example is shown in Figure 4-41.

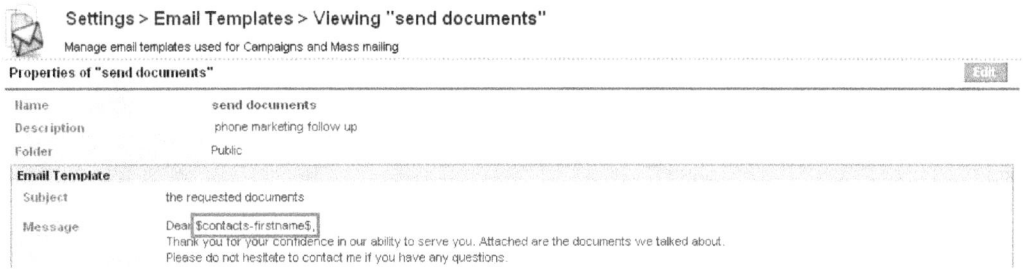

Figure 4-41: Email Template - Detail View

Note the merge field values highlighted in this figure. Merge field values are used to dynamically include data from your CRM into the mail.

In this example mail, the merge field value **$contacts firstname$** represents the first name of a contact.

You may include dynamic merge fields into your template at the Edit View as shown in Figure 4-42.

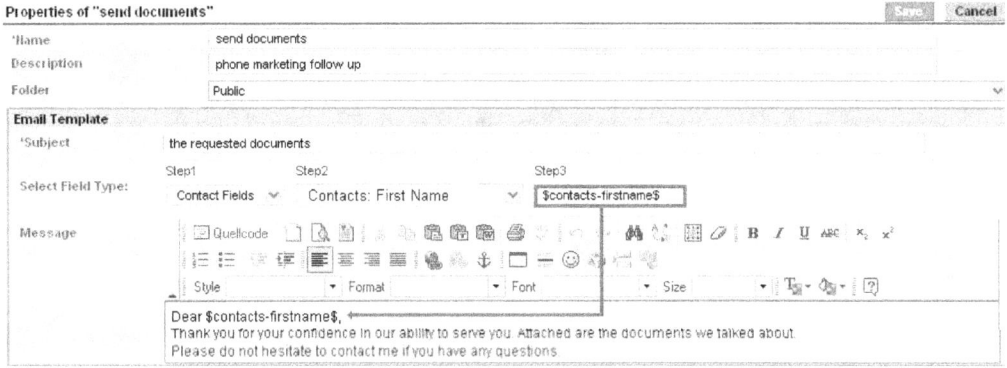

Figure 4-42: Email Template - Edit View

The merge field dialog supports you for defining the merge field syntax. You may include standard as well as custom fields as merge field. Use the copy and paste to enter the field codes.

You shall not mix field codes from different modules. For instance, if you use "Contact Fields" as shown in the figure you shall not add "Organization Fields" to this template.

All emails are going to be sent in the HTML format. You may use the HTML editor functions to design a special layout. You may also include HTML code which has been created by an external editor. But be careful and test your results, not all HTML code options are supported.

Click **[Save]** to transfer your template to the CRM system.

4.2.3.4 Company Details

If you use the CRM to create PDF outputs for your quotes, orders or invoices you must define the company information.

At the **Company Details** menu click the **[Edit]** button to enter company information as shown in Figure 4-43. You have to fill in all entry fields.

Figure 4-43: Company Information - Detail View

Make sure that the size of your company logo meets the space available for the PDF outputs. The logo must be provided in the *.png or *.jpg file format. The recommended size is about 150 x 60 pixels.

4.2.3.5 Mail Merge

The CRM system allows you to use the stored data to be merged with MS Word templates created at your office environment. This is very helpful if you frequently have to write letters, quotes or other standard documents.

To upload a template to the CRM system click the **[Add Template]** button at the **Mail Merge Template** menu as shown in Figure 4-44.

> The CRM system uses the company information for creating PDF output. If this information is not available at the time you create a PDF, an error message will be presented.

At this menu you see a list of all existing templates and you can mark and delete templates you do not need anymore.

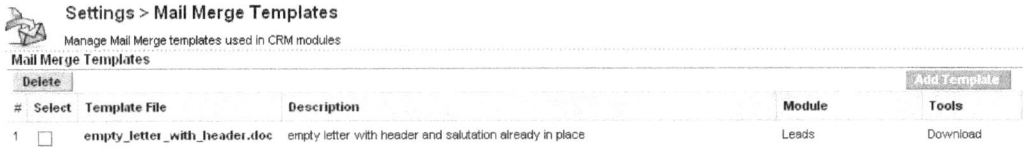

Figure 4-44: Mail Merge Template - List View

The edit view for new templates is shown in Figure 4-45. At this view you should provide a short description and select whether this template applies to Leads, Organizations, Contacts or Trouble Tickets. Then you have to provide the location of the template on your computer or network.

Figure 4-45: Mail Merge Template - Edit View

Click **[Save]** to transfer your template to the CRM system.

> Mail merge templates have to be created at our office environment first. You will need the MS Office Plugin provided with the CRM system. Please refer to Appendix Resources for further details.

4.2.4 Other Settings

With the help of the configuration functions you may specify your company information, configure the outgoing mail server, your backup access, and your default currencies.

4.2.4.1 Currencies

Click the **[Currency]** menu to set your system-wide currencies. You may add an unlimited number of currencies, by clicking the **[New Currency]** button as shown in Figure 4-46. You may also delete or edit exiting currencies by clicking the appropriate icons.

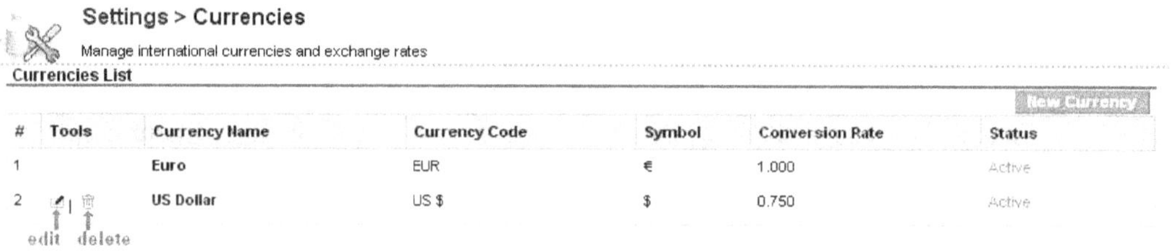

Figure 4-46: Currency Configuration

Table 4-11: Currency Information Fields

Type	Content
Currency Name:	The name of the currency, e.g. US Dollar.
Currency Code:	The short name of the currency, e.g. Dollar.
Currency Symbol:	Enter the symbol of the currency. This symbol will be used at the CRM for all price information, e.g. $.
Conversion Rate:	Enter the currency conversion rate in relation to the CRM basic currency. The basic currency is the first currency at your currency list.
Status:	You may set a currency as active or inactive. Inactive currencies cannot get assigned to users as described in section: User Management.

4.2.4.2 Tax Calculations

In all phases of the sales process, the CRM system considers all type of taxes which may apply to the sales of products or services. That may include local, state or federal taxes as well as special taxes. These taxes can be calculated individually for each product or service to be sold, or may be calculated for the whole.

Figure 4-47: Tax Setting - List View

You may refer to the article Product Details in Quotes for further information on the use of the tax settings. The CRM System may include taxes when calculating prices for quotes, orders or invoices. To change the settings of the existing taxes, click the **[Edit]** button at the **Tax Calculations** menu as shown in Figure 4-47.

To add new taxes use the **Add Tax** button. You might define as many additional taxes as you need. Enter your taxes in percent (%). Note that you cannot delete the default taxes as they are provided with the CRM system. However, you may deactivate not needed taxes by clicking the appropriate check box.

Click **[Save]** to transfer your tax settings to the CRM system.

4.2.4.3 Outgoing Server

If you want to send emails from the CRM system or if you want to receive notifications, you must configure the outgoing mail server.

Click **[Edit]** of the **Outgoing Server** menu to enter your mail server configuration as shown in Figure 4-48. Ask your service provider for the access data. Make sure that the server can be reached by the CRM system.

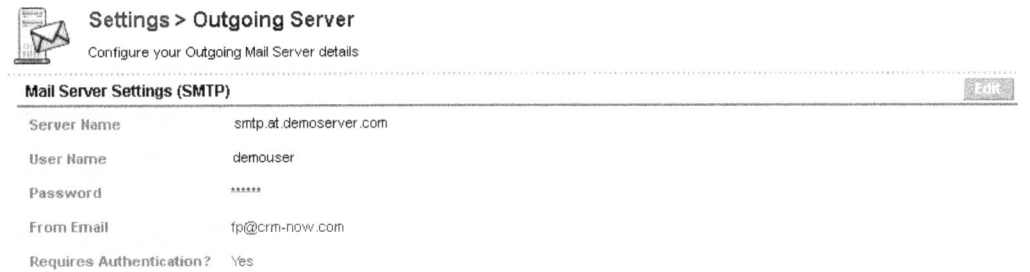

Figure 4-48: Outgoing Mail Server Configuration - Edit View

All CRM users will use the same outgoing mail server.

If a user sends an email by using the CRM, the user's email address as defined for each individual user at the user settings menu will be used as the sending email address.

However, if you have made an entry in the **From Email** field, this email address will be used as sending email address for all users and added to the **Reply to** content of your message.

4.2.4.4 Backup Server

The CRM system allows you to make a backup of the database locally at your own server hard disk or remotely at your FTP server. If configured, the CRM will make a backup of all data every time the **admin** user logs out.

Every backup will create a new file at the backup server. Make sure you that have enough disk space available and writing privileges for the directory selected. The names of these files are created automatically in the following format: "backup-<date>-<time>.sql".

Click the **[Edit]** button at the **Backup Server** menu to enter your server data as shown in Figure 4-49. Ask your FTP service provider for the access data. You may switch the backup on and off by marking the check box.

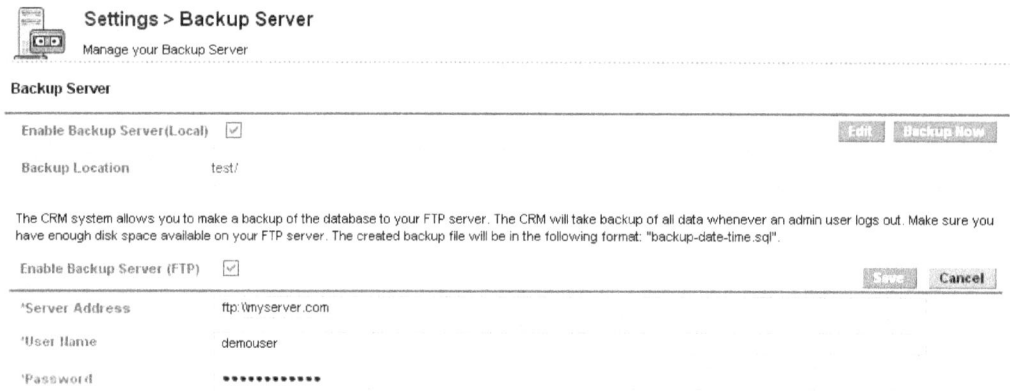

Figure 4-49: FTP Server Configuration - Detail View

Click **[Save]** to transfer your configuration to the CRM system.

4.2.4.5 Announcement

System administrators or users with administration privileges are provided with a function that enables them to send announcements to all CRM users. Such an announcement will be displayed at the top of the CRM system as illustrated in Figure 4-50.

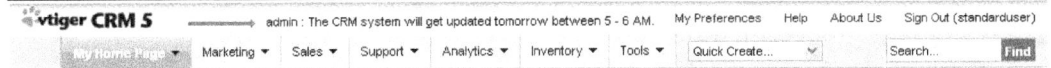

Figure 4-50: Announcement View

You may edit an announcement by clicking the **Update** button as presented in Figure 4-51.

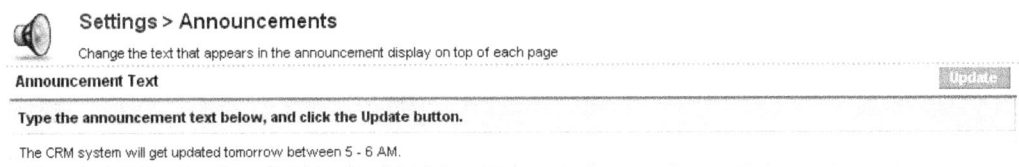

Figure 4-51: Announcement - Edit View

You may see the announcement when you leave the settings menu.

4.2.4.6 Assign Module Owners

Each CRM module has an owner. By default this owner is the user **admin**. At the current release, this function is only working for the trouble tickets in relation to the customer portal. Do not change the other settings!

You may assign the **Trouble Tickets** to another CRM user. When a ticket from the **Customer Portal** has been created, this ticket will be assigned to the corresponding module owner (user). The assigned user will receive an immediate email notification on the ticket creation. This is useful, for instance, for active trouble tickets management.

4.2.4.7 Proxy Server

If you company is using a proxy server to access the Internet, you can use the **Proxy Server Settings** menu as displayed in Figure 4-52 to enter server information. This might be needed by your CRM system when you use the RSS Reader or for accessing web pages. You need to enter all information.

Click [**Save**] to transfer the settings to the CRM system. The CRM will check whether a connection to the server has been established.

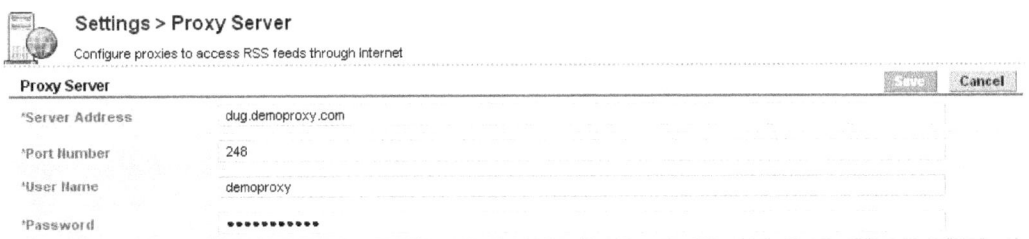

Figure 4-52: Proxy Server Settings - Edit View

4.2.4.8 Default Module View

The detail view of CRM entries is offering a **More Information** tab, which provides additional information related to an entry. You may switch to a **Singlepane** view. At this view the additional information will be listed below the master data as displayed in Figure 4-53.

Note that after switching the detail view for all CRM system modules changes.

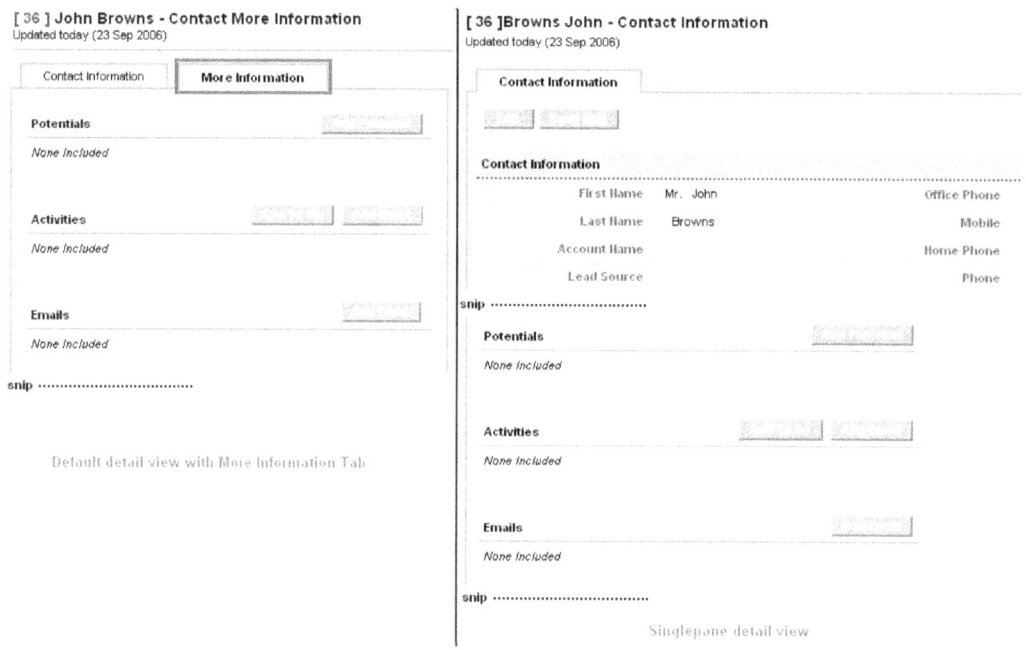

Figure 4-53: Default and Singlepane View Details

4.2.4.9 Inventory Terms & Conditions

You may store your default company terms and conditions in the CRM. Click **[Edit]** at the Inventory Terms & Conditions menu to open the edit view as shown in Figure 4-54.

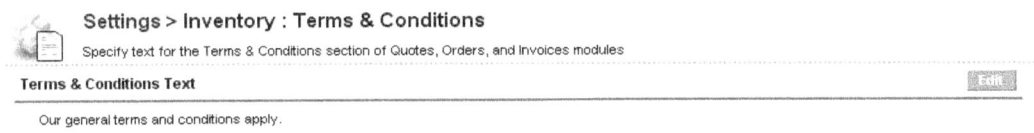

Figure 4-54: Inventory Terms & Conditions - Detail View

Enter your information. Click **[Save]** to transfer the information to the CRM. These terms and conditions will be available as default entries whenever you create a new quote, order or invoice.

4.2.4.10 Customize Record Numbering

While the CRM system uses its internal numbering system for all data. You can define your own numbering scheme for most of the modules.

You may define your numbering scheme by selecting the module first and entering your text for the prefix. Your start sequence must be a number which will increase by 1 every time you enter a new record.

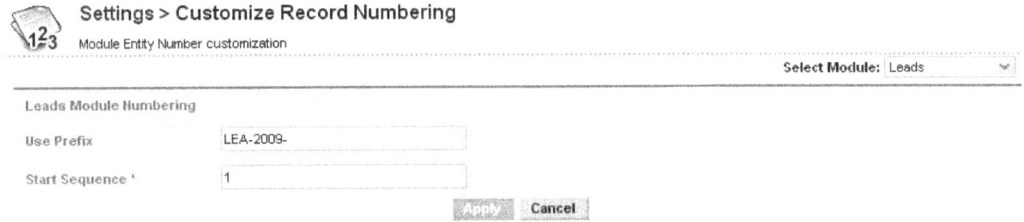

Figure 4-55: Customize Record Numbers

Figure 4-55 demonstrates a sample for Leads.

Click **[Save]** to make your numbering scheme active.

4.2.4.11 Mail Converter

The mail converter adds a capability to the CRM to scan a mail box automatically and to take action if the content of an incoming email meets certain criteria.

For example, you may have a specific email address for your support and the request that incoming emails should create a ticket in the CRM if these emails contain the string "support request". You may also use this scanner for mails which are generated by your web page in order to generate a contact in your CRM in case someone is interested to get more information about you offerings.

As a result of an email scan you have the following options:

- Create a trouble ticket: The SUBJECT of the email will become the title of the ticket. The BODY of the email will become the description of the ticket. Automatically the FROM email address is compared with existing Organization and Contact email addresses. If a match is found the trouble ticket will get associated with the existing Organization or Contact.
- Update a trouble ticket: The SUBJECT of the email will become the title of the ticket. The BODY of the email will become the description of the ticket.
- Add email to a Contact considering the FROM address
- Add email to a Contact considering the TO address
- Add email to an Organization considering the FROM address
- Add email to an Organization considering the TO address
- mark an email as READ as soon it has been scanned

To setup the mail scanner go to the Mail Scanner menu and click **[Edit]**. The incoming mail box configuration menu opens as shown in Figure 4-56. Note that this function is only available to mail boxes which provide IMAP (Internet Message Access Protocol) protocol capabilities. You may ask your Internet Service Provider for your IMAP access data and refer to http://en.wikipedia.org/wiki/Internet_Message_Access_Protocol for further information.

Enter your email box access data. By default the mail scanner is disabled. Make sure that you

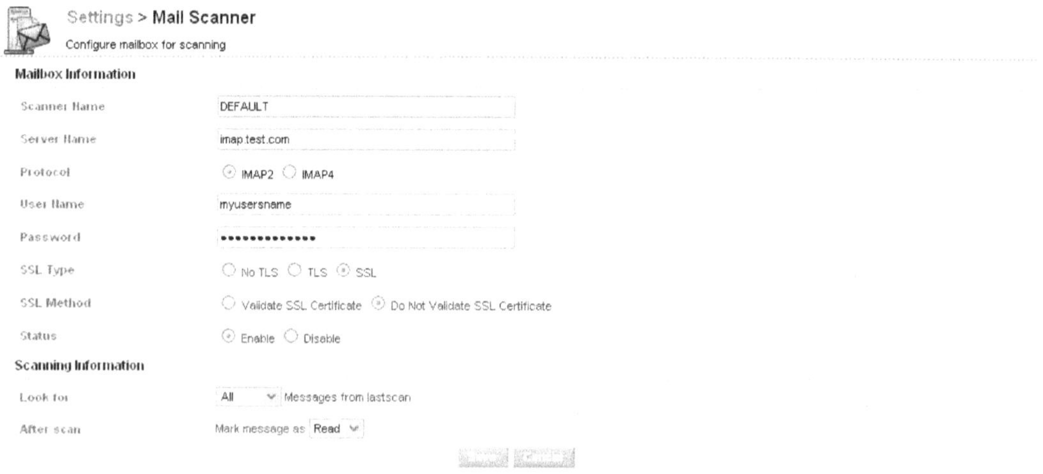

Figure 4-56: Mail Converter Configuration

enable the status before saving. When you click the [**Save**] button the CRM tries to connect to your mail box in order to verify proper operation. If you get the error message "Connecting to mailbox failed!" the mail box access information are not saved. Check your mail box settings and try again. If the CRM is able to communicate with your incoming mail box, further configuration options will be available as shown in Figure 4-57.

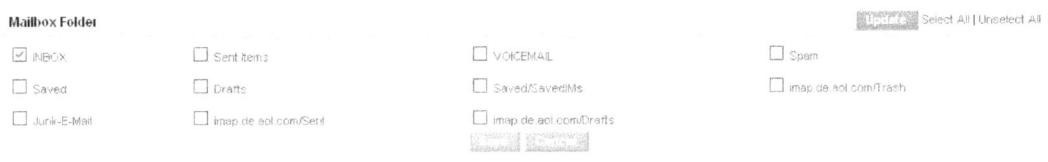

Figure 4-57: Mail Converter Detail View

By clicking the [**Select Folders**] button the CRM will display all mail folders available at your IMAP mail box as illustrated in Figure 4-58. You should disable the mail scan of folders which are not related to incoming emails by unmarking the check boxes.

Figure 4-58: Mail Converter Folders

By clicking the button [**Setup Rule**] button the CRM will allow you to setup one or multiple rules for your incoming emails. The Figure 4-59 illustrates possible settings. In this example a CRM ticket with the email content gets generated automatically if the subject of the email contains the text 'support request'. If you want that all emails from a certain mail box creates an action and do not include any conditions.

The condition may be just words or in case of a **Subject** also Regular Expressions, selectable as Regex. Regular Expressions are used for identifying strings of text, such as particular characters, words, or patterns of characters. Regular Expressions are powerful but not simple. You can't learn to use Regular Expressions from a brief overview and therefore these are not subject of this manual. For instance, the Regular Expression **/\bweb\b/i** would find the word **web** in the subject of an email. For a complete introduction to Regular

Expressions you may refer to the Wiki at http://en.wikipedia.org/wiki/Regular_expression, a Web Site like http://www.regular-expressions.info/, or other resources.

If you would like to set conditions you may use the following options:

- **From:** scan the text in the FROM field of the email address for match with the condition
- **To:** scan the text in the TO field of the email address for match with the condition
- **Subject:** scan the text in the SUBJECT field of the email for match with the condition, you may use one of the following conditions: Contains, Not contains, Equals, Not equals, Begins with, Not begins with or Regex
- **Body:** scan the text in the BODY field of the email for match with the condition, you may use one of the following conditions: Contains, Not contains, Equals, Not equals, Begins with, Not begins
- **Match:** if you have configured more than one conditions, you may select [all conditions] if all of the conditions should be met, or [any conditions] if at least one of the conditions should be met

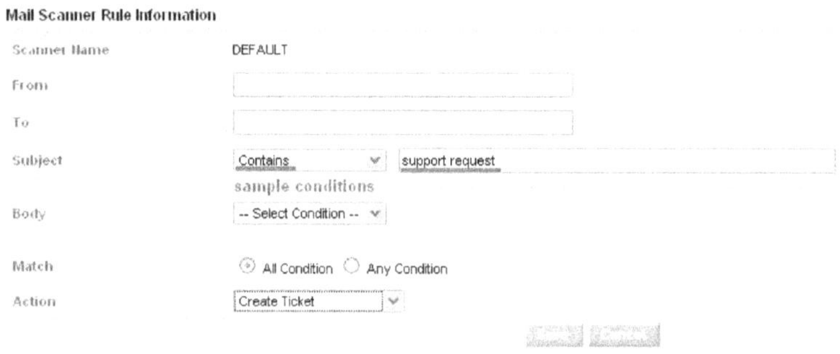

Figure 4-59: Mail Converter Rule Sample

Click **[Save]** to transfer the rule to the CRM system. You may setup one or multiple rules. If you have multiple rules it is sometimes necessary that you are able to set the order of a scan execution. This is done by changing the list order as illustrated in Figure 4-60.

When done the CRM is ready to scan your mail box every time you click the **Scan Now** button at the [**Mail Converter**] menu. Your first scan may take a little bit of time depending on the content of your mail box and the access speed.

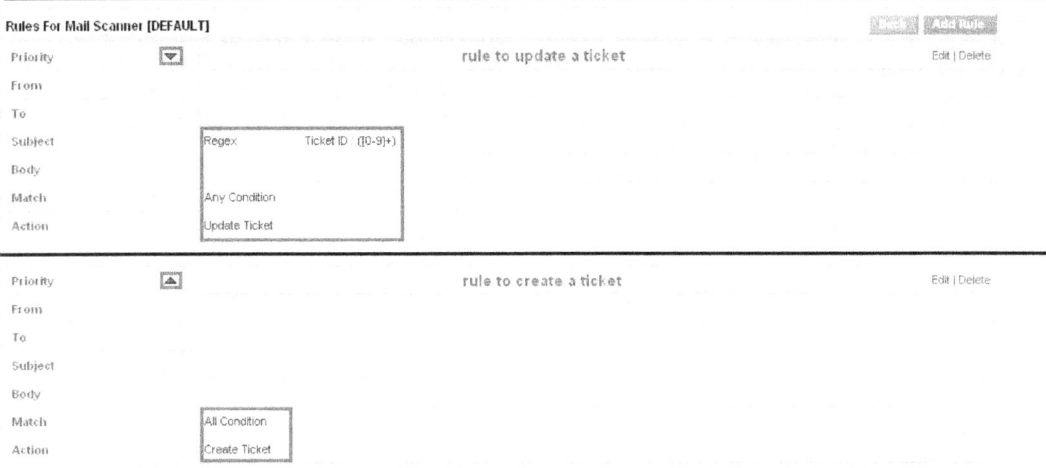

Figure 4-60: Mail Converter Priorities

It is also possible to have an automatic scan of your mail box. This must get configured during the CRM system installation and can't get accessed by a CRM user or administrator.

The example in Figure 4-60 illustrates how you could setup mail scanning conditions to create and to update tickets. This would be a proper mail scanner setup under the assumption that you have setup an email box for scanning and every incoming mail should either create a new ticket or update an existing ticket in CRM.

To create a ticket for all incoming emails you need to create a mail scanner rule as displayed in the lower part of this figure. All conditions fields are left blank, only the **Match** and the **Action** conditions are set. Whenever a mail comes in a new ticket will be created.

Each ticket in the CRM has a ticket number. This number should be part of the subject in reply message in order to bring the email in relation to the ticket. The procedure is illustrated at the left part in Figure 4-61.

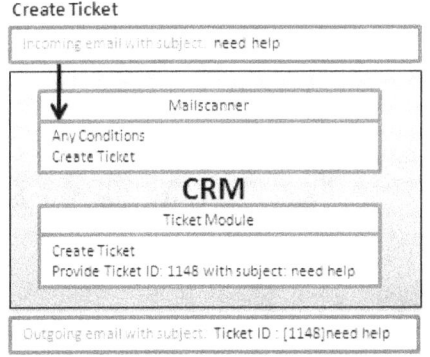
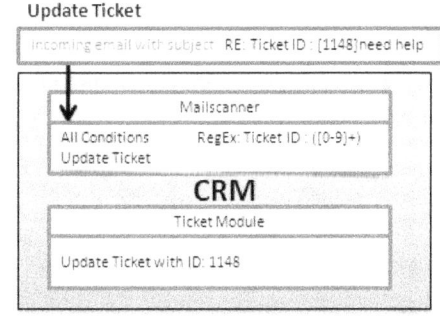

Figure 4-61: Mail Scan Workflow for Tickets

To update an existing ticket, you must set different conditions as illustrated in the upper part of Figure 4-60.

You need to define a **RegEx** condition in order to scan for a ticket number and set the **Match** and the **Action** conditions as illustrated. The workflow is illustrated in the right part of Figure 4-61.

As a last step make sure that the order of rules is set properly. You scanner must first check whether an existing ticket can be updated. If there is no ticket to update the second rule applies and a new ticket will get created.

4.2.4.12 Workflows

A workflow is a depiction of a sequence of operations, declared as work for the CRM system. You may setup such workflows in order to have the CRM doing some actions automatically. The execution of workflows consider conditions set by you and are triggered

- on the first saving a CRM record only.
- when the first time the conditions are met.
- every time a record is saved.
- every time a record is modified.

In the following the setup of a workflow is described for the Contacts module as an example. You may use the same procedure to create workflows for other CRM modules. Creating a workflow requires three steps:

First you need to create a new workflow by selecting the related CRM module and clicking the **[New Workflow]** button as shown in Figure 4-62. In the popup window you will be ask whether you want to create a new workflow from scratch or use an existing template. When you create a workflow the first time no templates are available. But you may create templates from your created workflows later.

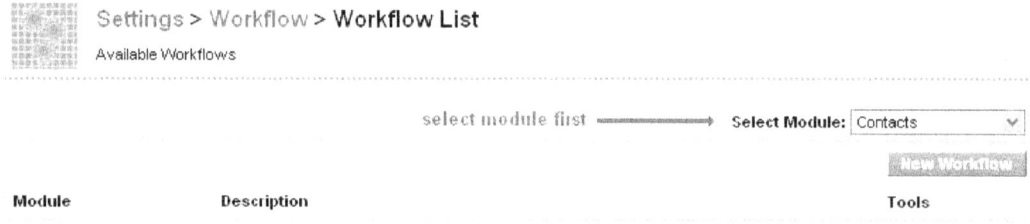

Figure 4-62: Create Workflow

After creation of a workflow you need to set a single or multiple conditions for the execution of the workflow. You have to set a running condition which defines an action on which a workflow will be executed. You may combine the trigger condition with a filter condition as illustrated in Figure 4-63.

Figure 4-63: Create Workflow Conditions

If you need conditions which look up the data before executing a workflow click the **[New Condition Group]** button. The first column let you select a field and the second column offers you the filter conditions which may get used with the selection. When you click the third column a new window opens as illustrated in Figure 4-64.

Figure 4-64: Workflow - Set Filter Value

Depending in your selection at the first column you may set a value as text, field or expression. The following table explains the details.

Table 4-12: Workflow - Filter Value Types

Type	Description
Raw Text:	This is the simplest form of a filter value. You may enter any text. This may lead you to a condition filter like 'Mailing City' *equals* 'Berlin'. For certain entry field types, like for instance a checkbox, the menu will provide the substitute values.
Field:	You may setup a value that references to another field. The menu offers you a substitute field as it used by the CRM internally. You could setup a filter like 'Mailing City' *equals* 'othercity'.
Expression:	This type allows you to combine a filter with a formula. Select the field first and the menu will display the possible formula operations. You may always use standard logical operations combined with special field type related operations as explained in the following table.

Table 4-13: Workflow - Formula Types

Formula	Description
arithmetic operations:	You may use the following arithmetic operations for all expressions: + : Addition - : Subtraction * : Multiplication / : Division
conditional operations:	You may setup a value which is based on If and else conditions. A formula may look like: *If* <condition> *then* <function> *else* <function> *end*
concat:	concat is the short form of concatenate. This is a string operation which assembles entries to one term. This may combine first and last name divided by a space character: *concat* (firstname, ' ',lastname)

Formula	Description
time_diffdays:	This formula type is only available for date fields. It provides the calculation of a date difference in days. You may add one or two parameters. For instance: *time_diffdays* (support_end_date,support_start_date) calculates the number of days between these two dates. *time_diffdays* (birthday) calculates the number of days between today and the birthday entry
time_diff:	This formula type is only available for date fields. Similar to the time_diffdays it provides a time difference but in seconds.
add_days:	This formula type is only available for date fields. It adds days to a given date with one or two parameters. For instance: *add_days* (birthday, 2) adds two days to the birthdate *add_days* (2) adds two days to the current date
sub_days:	This formula type is only available for date fields. It is similar to the add_days formula but provides a subtraction. For instance: *sub_days* (birthday, 2) subtracts 2 days from the birthdate

Click **[Save]** to transfer your workflow setup to the CRM.

The last step in setting up a workflow is the definition of a task which shall be executed when a workflow runs. The CRM supports the following types:

- Send Email: an email will be send automatically from the CRM if all conditions are met.
- Create ToDo: a task will be created and stored at the CRM automatically.
- Create Event: an event (call, meeting or a self-defined event) will be created and stored at the CRM
- Invoke Custom Function: Custom functions for workflows are complex functions designed to provide a special tasks. The original CRM comes only with one custom function called Update Inventory which is designed to set the inventory in your warehouse. This function can be used if you create a workflow for sales orders or invoices. You cannot create additional custom functions with the CRM GUI and should check with your CRM administrator whether further

custom functions are available.

Click **[New Task]** and select the task type. As an example Figure 4-65 illustrates a menu for an Event task. You have to give this task a title and a name, select the status and the type and you may add additional time conditions and content as shown in this figure.

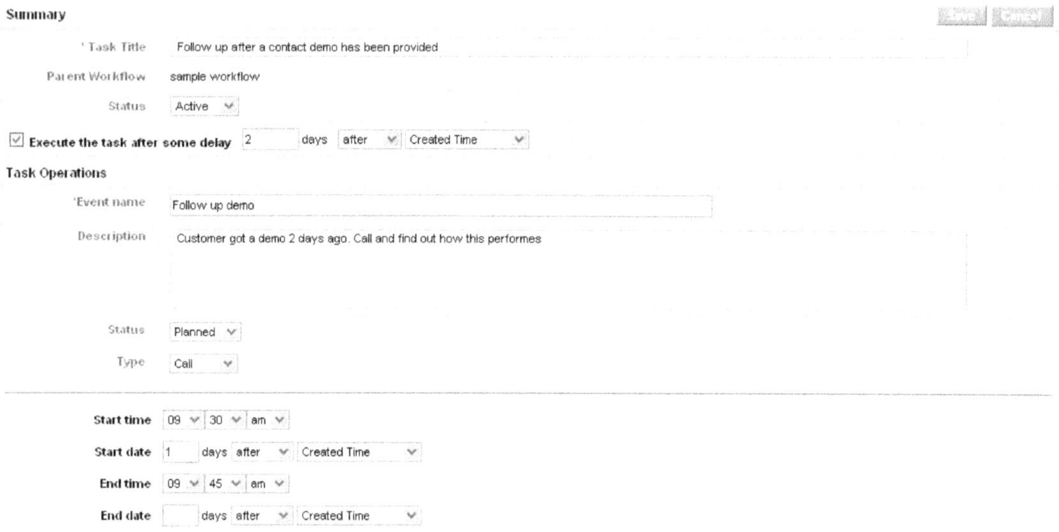

Figure 4-65: Workflow Task Sample

Note that each of the task types differs in the menu. Please refer to the corresponding sections in this manual for further information about the entry fields for a specific menu.

Click **[Save]** to transfer your tasks settings to the CRM and to get back to an overview menu that displays all the workflow conditions you have set.

4.2.4.13 Customer Portal

This menu is only available if you have installed the appropriate optional CRM package. With this the CRM system provides a feature that offers customers a limited access to your CRM system, to communicate with your company directly and to have access to customer related information. That includes but is not limited to:

- The access to CRM system FAQ's by a **Knowledge Base**. You may us this to provide release information or to answer common questions on the goods or services your company offers. Note that only information with the status **Published** will get displayed at the Customer Portal.
- The possibility to create and to track tickets.
- The possibility to access further information stored at the CRM such as Quotes, Invoices, Contact and Organization information as well as Product listings.

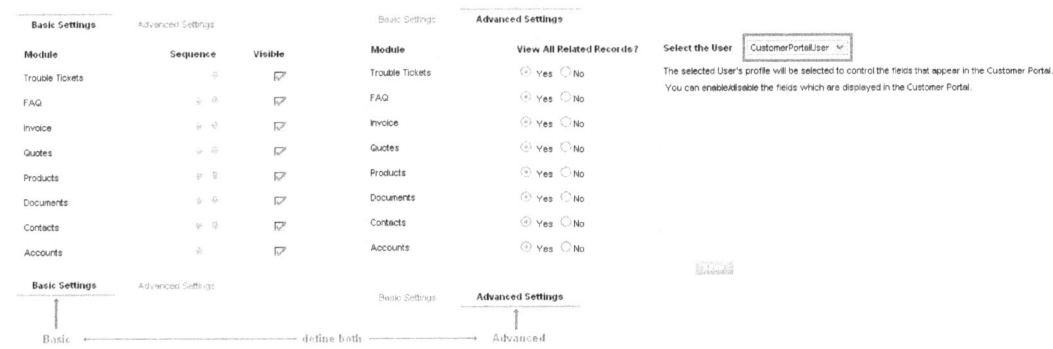

Figure 4-66: Customer Portal Settings

You may decide which information will be provided to the Customer Portal as illustrated in Figure 4-66. For a proper setup it is recommended that you create special CRM user who relates to a special customer portal profile. This can be used to define the fields to be displayed in the Customer Portal.

You may define who may access the customer portal by a special login procedure and a special URL. Ask your CRM administrator for this URL. The access is controlled by the contacts master data as described in 2.1.3 at page 24. Please refer to the **Customer Portal Manual** for further information, as listed in Appendix: Resources.

4.2.4.14 Configuration Editor

The CRM is running under certain setup conditions, stored in a file called config.inc.php, which you may modify by the Configuration Editor Menu, illustrated in Figure 4-67.

If you modify the settings, the changes become valid for all CRM users, depending on the menu item immediately or after the next login.

You need to know the server's resources before you can make a qualified modification. If your modifications to the settings exceed the server's capabilities they may become invalid, or in the worst case, generate error messages for CRM users.

Figure 4-67: Configuration Editor Menu

The following table explains the menu items.

Table 4-14: Configuration Menu Items

Menu	Description
Mini Calendar, World Clock and Calculator display:	You may remove these functions without any harm to other CRM functions if you do not need the related icons in the CRM's menu.

Menu	Description
Use RTE:	RTE is responsible for displaying the CRM's HTML Editor when you create a new message or text, applicable for instance to a new document or new email. If you switch this to false, the HTML editor will not be available anymore for the CRM and all text you have created before with this editor will get displayed in HTML Coding.
Help Desk Information:	The Help Desk related Information is used by the CRM when sending out automatic emails. You should modify this to fit your company's needs.
Max. Upload Size:	This entry relates to the maximum size of uploads to the CRM as you may perform it for instance for documents or email attachments. The maximum size depends on your server's resources and should only get increased when you are sure that your server has this capability.
Max. entries in List View:	This number controls the number of data sets you can see in a List View at once. Increasing this number, may increase the download time for a list.
Max. History Viewed:	This number controls the number of entries you see when you click the history icon at the Tools Area.
Default Module:	This entry controls the menu which is called after a login. The setting is valid for all CRM users. The standard value is Home.
Tex length in List View:	This is the number of characters displayed in a List View. If the length of an entry exceeds this number, the entry will get cut off.

4.2.4.15 ModTracker

The ModTracker allows you to add to the Detail View of CRM entries a History View menu. At this new menu you can see a collection of all actions that had been performed between an entries' Edit and Save operation. The following explains the functionality for the Contacts module. The same rules apply for the other modules.

If you enable the ModTracker for Contacts as shown in Figure 4-68 you will see the new menu entry in a Contact's detail view as illustrated in Figure 4-69.

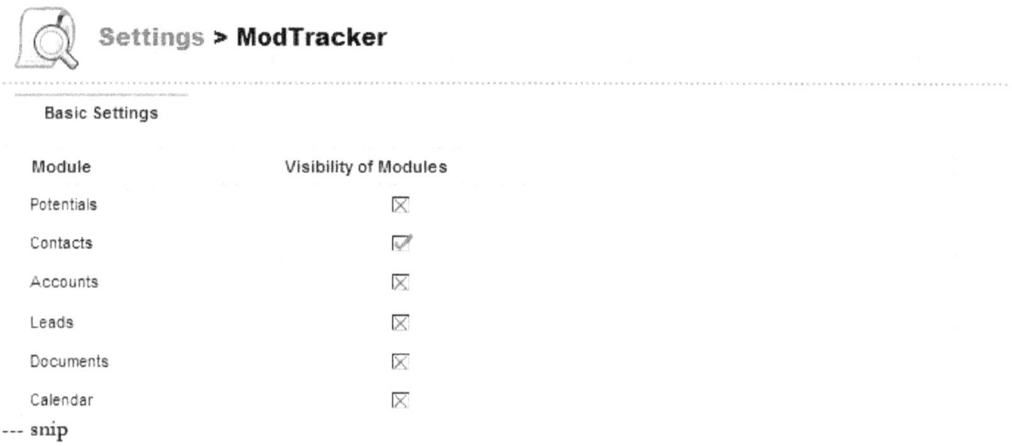

Figure 4-68: ModTracker Menu

Figure 4-69: View History in Detail View

By clicking the new **[View History]** menu you may see who has made a modification to a particular entry as illustrated in Figure 4-70. The menu also displays the name of the record, a time stamp and the details of the modification.

You may click the icons to go back and forward in the history.

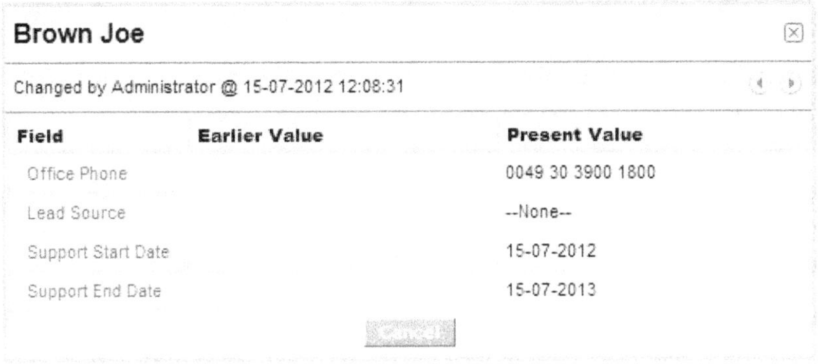

Figure 4-70: ModTracker History Sample

4.2.4.16 Scheduler

Your CRM System uses so called cron jobs as illustrated in Figure 4-71. Cron enables users to schedule jobs to run periodically at certain times.

The first setup of the cron jobs had been done during the CRM installation. The Scheduler menu allows you to modify the settings. Each cron job need system resources and therefore it is recommended that you set not needed jobs to InActive. To change the Status or Frequency, click the icon at Tools.

Figure 4-71: Scheduler Menu

If the Last Scan Started or Last Scan Ended information remains empty, the cron jobs do not work as expected and the server's setup must get checked.

4.2.4.17 Webforms

Webforms are software packages which make it possible to transfer data directly from a website to the CRM system. The following describes the mode of operation:

- A web designer integrates the available code into a website and generates a contact form. If necessary, adjustments of the design will be made.
- A potential customer types her/his data into the contact form at your website.
- The data of the potential customer are transferred to the CRM and generate a lead.
- The lead will be assigned to a CRM user for further treatment.

This module helps you to create code for your web site. The provided code includes all necessary parts for the transfer of data from a web based application to the CRM. The code is delivered in HTML. You will have to add PHP code to make your Webform secure. PHP is a scripting language which can be embedded in HTML sites and support its purposes. For further information on PHP check: www.php.net

In the Webforms menu click the icon to get to the setup menu, as illustrated in Figure 4-72. You need to give your form a unique name and you may add a description. When you select the Module the Field Information get filled with the fields available for this module automatically. It considers your field settings done at the Module Manager.

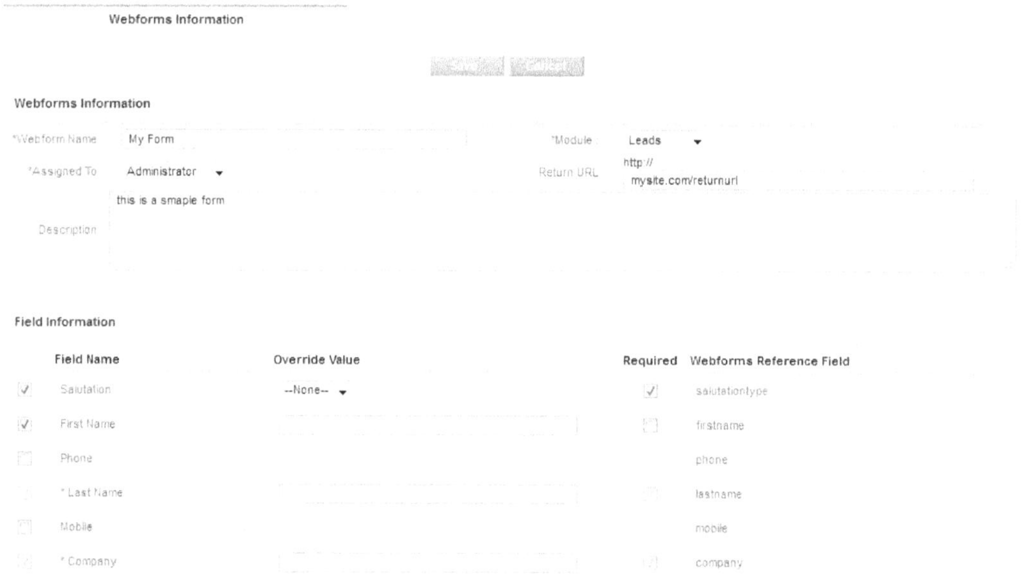

Figure 4-72: Webforms Setup Menu

The **Assigned To** field lists the CRM users and groups. You need to select one of these entries. The user or the user group will become the owner of the entries, generated by the Webform at your CRM.

The **Return URL** is optional. This URL can be the return address at your web site after the data are transmitted to the CRM.

Mark the checkboxes at the Field Information block you want to have at your web page to be filled out. Mandatory fields are already checked. The following table explains the Field Information columns.

Table 4-15: Webforms - Field Information

Column	Description
Fieldname:	These are the field names as you have it in your CRM menu.
Overwrite Value:	The information you enter here are becoming the default value for this field. You may use it for instance for internal information you want to store with every Webform entry.
Required:	If you mark the checkbox related to a field, this field becomes a mandatory entry at your Webform.
Reference field:	These are the field names the CRM uses internally. They will become the name of the field in your HTML form.

Click **[Save]** to transfer your information to the CRM. It opens the Detail View of your form. As illustrated in Figure 4-73 two new entries have been added to your menu.

Figure 4-73: Webforms - Detail View

The **Public Id** is a unique Webform identification number. This Id is used to identify your Webform to the CRM and should not get published.

The **Post URL** is used as a dummy entry in the final webform. This URL should get substituted by your real URL.

Click the **[Show Form]** button to see the HTML code generated. This code is the template for the code you may place at your website but needs 2 further customization to the entries highlighted in Figure 4-74.

Figure 4-74: Webforms - Code

1. Set a proper URL: In the figure above you see the URL which is called by the HTML form. This URL must be available at your CRM system.

2. Replace the publicid field: The Webforms generator places the publicid in a hidden HTML field. It exposes your secret key to the public. This may get used by hackers to get unauthorized access to the CRM system and should be avoided. You may find a better approach at the following URL:

https://wiki.vtiger.com/index.php/Developers_How_To%27s#Simple_example_for_a_sec ured_form_which_adds_a_lead_to_the_CRM

Finally, place the generated code at your web page and add your own design.

5 Administrations Examples

This appendix discusses the security setup for example organizations and explains what individual users are allowed to do on the CRM system under certain conditions. These examples do not include all possibilities for configuring the CRM system based on a company's needs. However, the principal functions of the security features are covered so that an administrator might quickly become capable to create his or her own setup.

a. Example I: Organizing a very small organization

The following configuration examples are based on a sales team as illustrated in Figure 5-1.

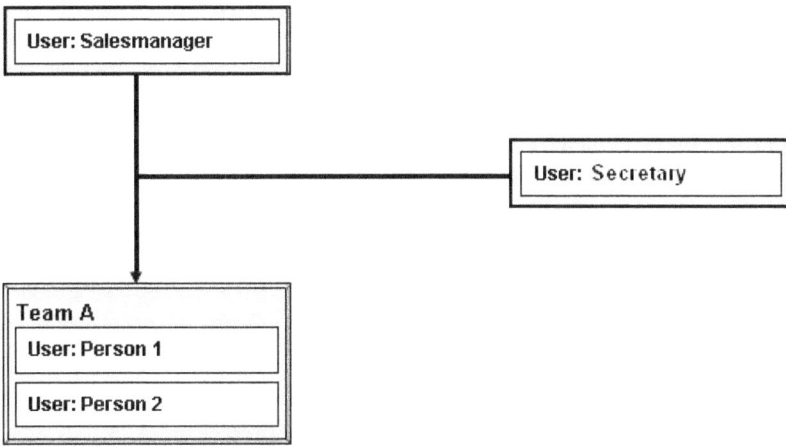

Figure 5-1: Example I Sales Team

5.1 Example I

For the first example settings we want to have the following rules implemented for Leads:

- Person 1 and Person 2 have the permission to create Leads that are owned by Person 1 or Person 2.
- Person1 will have no access privileges to Leads from Person 2 and vice versa.
- The Sales manager has all access privileges to all Leads.
- The secretary has no privileges to access Leads. The following settings are necessary:

Create one common profile for Person 1, Person 2 and the Sales manager:

We need one profile, called Sales which should include all CRUD privileges for Leads. Make sure that the Global Privileges are disabled

Create one profile for the Secretary:

Based on the **Sales** profile create a new profile, called **Secretaryprofile** where the access to the Leads module is disabled.

Create three roles:

We need one role for the Sales manager, called **Sales Manager**, and one subordinated role for Person 1 and 2, called **Sales Men**. All roles are based on the **Sales** profile.

In addition, we need another subordinated role for the secretary, called **Secretary Sales** based on the **Secretaryprofile** that reports to the sales manager.

Set the sharing access:

At the **Organization-level Sharing Rules** menu set the rules for Leads to **private**.

Since role of the Sales manager is superior to the role of Person 1, 2 the Sales manager has all CRUD privileges to the data of Person 1 and Person2. If Person 1 or Person 2 creates a

> Always remember: If you make changes to the sharing rules, you must hit the [**Recalculate**] button to make your changes valid!

Lead, the owner gets assigned. If Person1 is assigned as owner of a Lead, Person 1 and the Sales manager can access and modify this Lead. If the ownership is changed to any one member of the team (Person 1 or Person 2) then only this person and the Sales manager can access the Lead. The secretary does not see any Lead data.

5.1.1 Example I: settings with groups

As another example setting we want to have the following rules implemented for Leads:

- Person 1 and Person 2 have the permission to create Leads that are owned by Person 1 or Person 2 or by the team.
- If a Lead is owned by a single Person the other team member will have no access privileges to this Lead.
- The Sales manager has all access privileges to all Leads.
- The Secretary has all access privileges to Leads owned by the team.

In order to implement these rules you have several options. These options are based on the following common settings:

Create one common profile for Person 1 and 2 and the Sales manager:

We need only one profile, called **Sales** which should include all CRUD privileges for Leads. Make sure that the **Global Privileges** are disabled.

Create two roles:

We need one role for the Sales manager, called **Sales Manager**, and one subordinated role for Person 1, 2 and the secretary, called Sales Men. Both roles are based on the Sales profile. Since the role of the Sales manager is superior to the role of the other users the Sales manager has all CRUD privileges.

Create one group:

Option 1:

> Create a group of users, called **Team A**. Include the Person 1 and Person 2 and the secretary user. We have to include the Sales Manager because groups of users are independent to the role-based hierarchy and we will need access to the Leads assigned to Team A.

Option 2:

> Create a group of role & subordinates, called **Team A**. Include the role of the Sales Manager.

Option 3:

> Create a group of roles, called **Team A**. Include the role **Sales Manager**, the role **Sales Men**.

Set the sharing access:

At the **Organization-level Sharing Rules** menu set the rules for Leads to **private**.

If Person 1 or Person 2 creates a Lead the owner gets assigned. If Team A is assigned as owner of the Lead, Person 1, Person 2, the Sales manager as well as the secretary can access the Lead. If the ownership is changed to any one member of the group (Person 1 or Person 2), then only this person and the Sales manager can access the Lead.

> Always remember: If you make changes to the sharing rules, you must hit the **[Recalculate]** button to make your changes valid!

5.1.2 Example I: settings with sharing access

As another example we want to have the following rules implemented for Leads:

- Person 1 and Person 2 have the permission to create Leads that are owned by Person 1 or Person 2.
- If a Lead is owned by a single Person another team member will have read only access privileges to this Lead.
- The Sales manager has all access privileges to all Leads.
- The secretary has View only privileges to access Leads.

In order to implement these rules I have to implement the following settings:

Create one common profile for Person 1 and 2 and the Sales manager:

We need one profile, called Sales that should include all CRUD privileges for Leads. Make sure that the Edit All check box under Global Privileges is disabled.

Create one profile for the Secretary:

Based on the Sales profile create a new profile, called **Secretaryprofile** where the access to Leads is set to View only.

Create three roles:

We need one role for the Sales manager, called Sales Manager, and one subordinated role for Person 1 and 2, called **Sales Men**. All roles are based on the **Sales** profile.

In addition, we need another subordinated role for the secretary, called **Secretary Sales** based on the **Secretaryprofile** that reports to the Sales manager.

Global Access Privileges:

We need to set the global privileges for Leads to Public Read Only.

Since the role of the Sales manager is superior to the role of Person 1, 2 the Sales manager has all CRUD privileges to the data of Person 1 and Person2. If Person 1 or Person 2 creates a Lead the owner gets assigned. If Person1 is assigned as owner of a Lead, Person 1 and the Sales manager can access and modify this Lead.

> **Always remember:** If you make changes to the sharing rules, you must hit the **[Recalculate]** button to make your changes valid!

If the ownership is changed to any one member of the team (Person 1 or Person 2) then only this person and the Sales manager can access the Lead. The secretary has read only privileges to all Lead data.

5.2 Example II

This example demonstrates how the access to certain data can be controlled by a combination of groups with sharing rules.

Let us assume we have a sales team as displayed as an organization chart in Figure 5-2. The sales manager is the supervisor for Person 1 to 4, all organized in Team A and B, as well as the sales assistant. This sales assistant supports the sales teams.

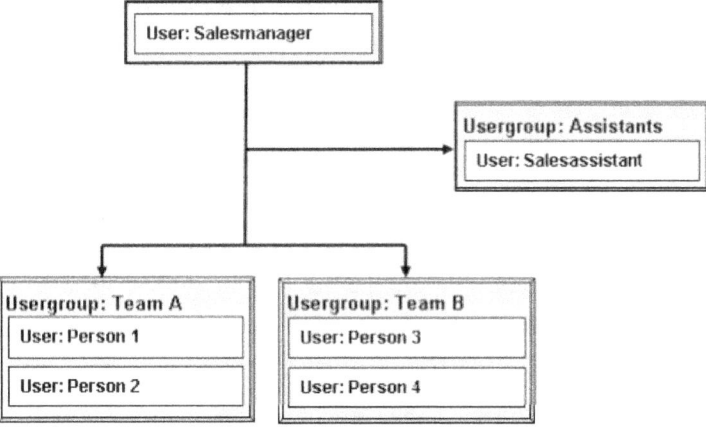

Figure 5-2: Example II Sales Team

5.2.1 Example II: Settings primary based on groups

Let us assume we want to have the following rules for Leads implemented.

- People 1-4 have the permission to create Leads which are owned by any person or by the Team A or B.
- Person 1-4 have Read/Write privileges to all Leads regardless who owns it.
- The Sales assistant has Read/Write privileges to Leads of the Team A only and cannot access the Leads of Team B.
- The Sales manager has all access privileges to all Leads.

In order to implement these rules I set the following privileges:

Create two profiles:

We need one profile for Persons 1-4 and the Sales manager, called **Sales** that should include all CRUD privileges. In addition, we need a profile for the Sales assistant called **Assistance** which should have the **Edit all** checkbox under Global Privileges deactivated.

> Since we have set the Global Access Privileges for Leads to **private**, Rules 4 and 5 are necessary to allow that the group members of Team A and B can see each other's Leads.

Besides, the **Delete** permission for the Leads module must be deactivated, too.

Create three roles:

We need one role for the Sales manager called **Manager**, one subordinated role for the Sales assistant called **Salesassistant** and one subordinated role for all Persons 1-4 called **SalesAll**.

The roles **Manager** and **SalesAll** are based on the **Sales** profile whereas the role **Salesassistant** is based on the **Assistance** profile.

> As described in section 4.2.1.5 sharing rules cannot be specified to share data between users. Since we want to use sharing rules for the Sales assistant, we have to create an additional group with only one member.

Create three groups of users:

We create a group called **Team A** with the members Person 1 and Person 2 and a group called **Team B** with the members Person 3 and Person 4. We create a group called **Assistant** with the user Sales assistant as the only member.

At Default Organization Sharing Access we set the Global Access Privileges for "Leads" to Private.

This will cause that users cannot access other users Leads.

Set Custom Sharing Rules for Leads:

1. Leads of Group **Team A** can be accessed by Group **Team B**; we set the access privilege with Read/ Write permission.

2. Leads of Group **Team B** can be accessed by Group **Team A**; we set the access privilege with Read/ Write permission.

3. Leads of Group **Team A** can be accessed by Group **Assistant**; we set the access privilege with Read/Write permission.

4. Leads of Group **Team A** can be accessed by Group **Team A**; we set the access privilege with Read/ Write permission.

5. Leads of Group **Team B** can be accessed by Group **Team B**; we set the access privilege with Read/ Write permission.

As described in section 4.2.1.5 sharing rules cannot be specified to share data between users. Since we want to use sharing rules for the Sales assistant, we have to create an additional group with only one member.

5.2.2 Example II: Settings primary based on roles

As a modification to the example above let us assume we want to have the same rules for Leads implemented:

- Person 1-4 have the permission to create Leads that are owned by any person or team.
- Person 1-2 have Read/Write privileges to all Leads owned by Person 1-2 and Team A. They have Read only permissions to Leads owned by Person 3-4 or Team B.
- Person 3-4 have Read/Write privileges to all Leads owned by Person 3-4 and Team B. They have Read only permissions to Leads owned by Person 1-2 or Team A.
- The Sales assistant has Read privileges to all Leads.
- The Sales manager has all access privileges to all Leads

In order to implement these rules we set the following privileges:

Create one common profile for all Persons, the Sales assistant and the Sales manager:

We need only one profile, called **Sales** that should have the **Edit all** check box under **Global Privileges** deactivated.

Create four roles:

1. We need one role for the Sales manager called **Manager**, based on the **Sales** profile.

2. We need one subordinated role for the Sales assistant called **Salesassistant**, based on the Sales profile.

3. We need one subordinated role for the Person1 and Person2 called **Team A**, based on the Sales profile.

4. We need one subordinated role for the Person3 and Person4 called **Team B**, based on the Sales profile.

As a result, the roles **Salesassistant**, **Team A**, and **Team B** are on an equal hierarchical level subordinated to the **Manager** role.

Create three groups of users:

We create a group called **Team A** with the members Person 1 and Person 2 and a group called **Team B** with the members Person 3 and Person 4. Note that the Sales manager has to be included in both groups since groups of users are independent of the role-based hierarchy and he will need access to the Leads assigned to **Team A** as well as **Team B**. We create a group called **Assistant** with the user Sales assistant as the only member.

At Default Organization Sharing Access we set the Global Access Privileges for "Leads" to Private:

This will cause that users cannot access other users Leads.

Set Custom Sharing Rules for Leads:

1. Leads of Role Team A can be accessed by Role Team B; we set the access privilege with Read Only permission.

2. Leads of Role Team B can be accessed by Role Team A; we set the access privilege with Read Only permission.

3. Leads of Role Team A can be accessed by Role Salesassistant; we set the access privilege with Read Only permission.

4. Leads of Role Team B can be accessed by Role Salesassistant; we set the access privilege with Read Only permission.

5. Leads of Role Manager can be accessed by Role Salesassistant; we set the access privilege with Read Only permission.

6. Leads of Role Team A can be accessed by Role Team A; we set the access privilege with Read/ Write permission.

7. Leads of RoleTeam B can be accessed by Role Team B; we set the access privilege with Read/ Write permission.

6 Administration FAQ

How to delete users, groups, profiles and roles:

If you delete a user, group, profile or role you will be asked for a new owner of the data. After selection the data will be moved to the new owner and will not be lost.

How to change a user's login name:

You cannot change the login name of a user directly. Instead, create a new user with a new login name and delete the old user. During deletion transfer all data of the old user to the new user.

How to restrict users sharing access:

If you have set everything based on the rules and tips provided and you still not get the desired results please check the following:

- Have you set the default organisation sharing access to private?
- Have you disabled View All and Edit All at the Global Permissions for profiles used?
- Have you clicked on the Recalculate button after making changes to the organization sharing access?
- Have you disabled the admin option for the users?

The CRM system checks the security system in the following order:

The **Global Privileges** are checked first. If the **Global Privileges** are enabled, no other security check will be done. Depending on the settings, any user may view and edit all the data of the CRM System, except the **Settings** module. At the same time the profile permission overrides the sharing rules, because the CRM system will not include the sharing rules into considerations.

If the **Global Privileges** are disabled, the system will check for the **Tab Privileges at the Profiles**. If the **Tab Privileges** are disabled, a user cannot view a particular module. At the same time the profile permission also overrides the sharing rules. This is because whatever permission you have in the sharing rules, this will not be taken into considerations if you do not have access to a particular module in first place.

If the **Tab Privileges** are available, this means that a current user can view a particular model. Now the CRM system checks for the settings of the **Sharing Rules**.

How to include contacts into a campaign:

Follow these steps if you want to associate a list of contacts to particular campaign:

1. at the Contacts List View:

    - If you do have contacts already in your CRM import your contacts (see section: Export and Import of CRM Data).

    - Create a custom view for the imported contacts (see section: Customize Lists).

2. at the Campaign List View:

    - Create a campaign.

    - In campaign detail view, scroll down to the Contacts related list (or select the **More Information** tab).

    - In Contacts related list there are three options: Load List | Select Contact | Add Contact

    - Load List: for associating contacts in bulk from the custom view. Select your required custom view to load your contacts list.

    - Select Contact: for selecting a few contacts from the available contact list.

    - Add Contact: for adding new contact on-the-fly.

    - Select the contacts you want to include into your campaign.

How to create additional events to meetings/calls:

If you want to add other event types you need to add such an type to the events picklist. As a user with admin privileges goto the **Picklist Editor** and select the **Events** module. Add your event type to the picklist.

7 Appendix Resources

The quantity of information about vtiger CRM is growing on a daily basis. This appendix strives to provide both a complete bibliography of the references mentioned explicitly in this book, and a sampling of resources for additional information on vtiger CRM and on CRM in general. Although not all of these resources are focused on vtiger CRM specifically, they still provide helpful information for vtiger CRM users.

Latest Versions of this Manual

The latest version of this manual can be obtained from the document download page at: http://www.vtiger-hilfe.de

Resources for Resources

Easily the largest and most up-to-date list of other vtiger CRM resources can be found on the vtiger Web page:

http://www.vtiger.com.

vtiger extensions to be used with the Module Manager can be found at the vtiger's Market Place page:

https://www.vtiger.com/add-ons/.

Other Material on vtiger CRM components.

vtiger hosts a community page that provide installation and operational descriptions about the CRM and its extensions at http://wiki.vtiger.com. Here you will find:
- vtiger CRM installation manuals
- additional administration and user manuals
- manuals for the CRM extensions such as the Outlook Plugin, Office Plugin, Customer Portal, Thunderbird Extension and Firefox Extension
- Administration manuals for technical issues
- How Tos

International vtiger community

There is a large international community that contributes to the vtiger CRM system. You may check out the following links for other documents or contributions:

- France: http://www.vtiger.fr/
- Germany: http://www.vtiger-hilfe.de
- Italy: http://www.vtiger.it
- Netherlands: http://vtiger-nl.org/
- Poland: http://www.vtiger.org.pl/
- Russia: http://www.vtiger.ru/ and http://myvtiger.kostigoff.net/
- Spain: http://www.vtigercrm.es/

This list might be incomplete since the vtiger community is growing fast. Please contact the author at vtiger- manual@crm-now.com if you know other references to be included in the next manual revision.

UTF-8 coding

The CRM system uses the UTF-8 format to store data. The following links may help you to understand this format and to use it when you import or export data.

- The online Wikipedia explains everything what you know about UTF-8: http://en.wikipedia.org/wiki/UTF-8
- Notepad++ is a generic editor you can use to convert data from and to UTF-8 http://sourceforge.net/projects/notepad-plus/
- vtiger tool for UTF-8 conversion: http://www.vtiger.com/index.php?option=com_content&task=view&id=163&Itemid=183
- a collection of other converting tools for UTF-8: http://dataconv.org/apps_unicode_utf8.html

List of Figures

Figure 1-1: Login Screen 10
Figure 1-2: CRM Home Page 11
Figure 1-3: Screen Top Area 12
Figure 1-4: Preferences - User Login & Role 13
Figure 1-5: Preferences - More Information 14
Figure 1-6: Preferences - User Advanced Option 15
Figure 2-1: New Lead - Basic Information 20
Figure 2-2: New Organization – Master Data 21
Figure 2-3: Call Organization Memberships 22
Figure 2-4: Display Organization Hierarchy 23
Figure 2-5: New Contact – Master Data 24
Figure 2-6: Contact List View Import/Export 26
Figure 2-7: Contacts Import, Steps 1-3 27
Figure 2-8: Contacts Import, Step 3 28
Figure 2-9: Contacts Import, Step 4 29
Figure 2-10: Contacts Import, Results 30
Figure 2-11: Contacts Import, Data Review 30
Figure 2-12: Export Selection 31
Figure 2-13: Calendar - Hour View 36
Figure 2-14: Calendar - New Event 37
Figure 2-15: Calendar - Event Reminder 38
Figure 2-16: Calendar - Repeat Events 39
Figure 2-17: Calendar - Event Relations 39
Figure 2-18: Calendar - New Task / ToDo 40
Figure 2-19: Calendar Settings 41
Figure 2-20: Calendar - Hour View 41
Figure 2-21: Lead - List View 44
Figure 2-22: Lead Detail View - Master Data 45
Figure 2-23: Lead Detail View - More Information 46
Figure 2-24: Opportunity - Create View 47
Figure 2-25: Opportunity Detail View - Master Data 48
Figure 2-26: Opportunity Detail View - More Information 49
Figure 2-27: Quote - Edit View 51
Figure 2-28: Quotes - Product Details with Individual Tax Mode 53
Figure 2-29: Quotes - Product Details with Group Tax Mode 53
Figure 2-31: Sales Order - edit view for sales order and addresses information 58
Figure 2-32: Sales Order - Edit view for recurring invoice information 59

Figure 2-33: Purchase Order - Create View for purchase order and address information blocks 60
Figure 2-34: Invoice - Detail View 62
Figure 2-34: Campaigns - List View 64
Figure 2-36: Campaign -Edit View 64
Figure 2-37: Campaign - Detail View - More Information 65
Figure 2-38: Products - Create View - Master Data 67
Figure 2-39: Display of multiple images for products 69
Figure 2-40: Product - Detail View - More Information 70
Figure 2-41: Select Products from Bundle 71
Figure 2-41: New Price Book Create View 71
Figure 2-43: Price Books - Product Selection List 72
Figure 2-44: Vendor - Edit View - Master Data 72
Figure 2-45: Vendor - More Information 73
Figure 2-46: Service - Create View - Master Data 74
Figure 2-47: Service Contract- Create View - Master Data 76
Figure 2-48: Asset - Create View - Master Data 77
Figure 2-49: Project - Create View - Master Data 78
Figure 2-50: Project Milestone - Create View - Master Data 79
Figure 2-51: Project Task - Create View - Master Data 80
Figure 3-1: Create a custom filter for a list view 81
Figure 3-2: Create Custom List - Edit View 82
Figure 3-3: Approve Custom View 83
Figure 3-4: Record Change Indicator 83
Figure 3-5: List View - Basic Search 84
Figure 3-6: List View - Advanced Search 84
Figure 3-7: List View - Mass Edit 85
Figure 3-8: List View - Mailer Export 86
Figure 3-9: Duplicate Search Result 87
Figure 3-10: List View - Duplicate Search 87
Figure 3-11: Duplicate Merge and Removal 88
Figure 3-12: Tag Cloud 88
Figure 3-13: Chat View 90
Figure 3-14: Documents - Default Folder 91
Figure 3-15: Documents - Create View 92
Figure 3-16: Recycle Bin - List View 93
Figure 3-17: Mass Mailing Selection 94
Figure 3-18: Compose Email Menu 95
Figure 3-19: Mail Manager - IMAP Settings 97

Figure 3-20: Mail Manager - Menu 97
Figure 3-21: Mail Manager - Message Detail View 98
Figure 3-22: Mail Manager - Compose Menu 98
Figure 3-23: Email Menu 99
Figure 3-24: Incoming Mail Server Details 99
Figure 3-25: Lead List View 103
Figure 3-26: Lead Detail View - Master Data 104
Figure 3-27: Convert leads menu 105
Figure 3-28: Opportunities List View 106
Figure 3-29: Trouble Ticket - Edit View 109
Figure 3-30: Trouble Ticket - List View 109
Figure 3-31: Trouble Ticket - Detail View - Master Data 110
Figure 3-32: FAQ - Edit View 112
Figure 3-33: Dashboard 113
Figure 3-34: Reports Home 114
Figure 3-35: Report Detail View 115
Figure 3-36: New Report - Detail View 115
Figure 4-1: Enable administrator access 120
Figure 4-2: Users, Roles and Profiles Relations 122
Figure 4-3: Group of Users - Example 125
Figure 4-4: Group of Roles - Example 126
Figure 4-5: Roles - Hierarchy Example 126
Figure 4-6: Group of Roles with Subordinates - Example 127
Figure 4-7: Sample Hierarchy for Groups 127
Figure 4-8: Additional Settings - Icon 128
Figure 4-9: CRM Users - List View 131
Figure 4-10: CRM Users - Detail View 133
Figure 4-11: Roles - Company Hierarchy Example 135
Figure 4-12: Role - Edit View 135
Figure 4-13: Profiles - List View 136
Figure 4-14: New Profile - Step 1 136
Figure 4-15: New Profile - Step 2 137
Figure 4-16: Groups - List View 138
Figure 4-17: Groups - Detail View 138
Figure 4-18: Group - Create View 139
Figure 4-19: Global Access Privileges - List View 140
Figure 4-20: Fields Manager for Calendar 144
Figure 4-21: Audit Trail - Configuration Menu 144
Figure 4-22: Audit Trail - Report 145

Figure 4-23: User Login History 145
Figure 4-24: Installing New CRM Module 146
Figure 4-25: Module Manager - Standard Modules 147
Figure 4-26: Layout Editor 147
Figure 4-27: Custom Field Definition 149
Figure 4-28: Map Lead Custom Fields 151
Figure 4-29: Tool Tip - Sample View 152
Figure 4-30: Tool Tip - FAQ Menu 152
Figure 4-31: Field Formulas in Module Manager 152
Figure 4-32: Field Formulas - Edit View 153
Figure 4-33: Studio - Picklist Editor 154
Figure 4-34: Picklist Dependency - List View 156
Figure 4-35: Picklist Dependency - Create View 156
Figure 4-36: Picklist Dependency - Concatenation Menu 157
Figure 4-37: Menu Editor - Edit View 158
Figure 4-38: Notification Schedulers - List View 159
Figure 4-39: Inventory Notifications 160
Figure 4-40: Email Templates - List View 160
Figure 4-41: Email Template - Detail View 161
Figure 4-42: Email Template - Edit View 161
Figure 4-43: Company Information - Detail View 162
Figure 4-44: Mail Merge Template - List View 163
Figure 4-45: Mail Merge Template - Edit View 163
Figure 4-46: Currency Configuration 164
Figure 4-47: Tax Setting - List View 165
Figure 4-48: Outgoing Mail Server Configuration - Edit View 165
Figure 4-49: FTP Server Configuration - Detail View 166
Figure 4-50: Announcement View 167
Figure 4-51: Announcement - Edit View 167
Figure 4-52: Proxy Server Settings - Edit View 167
Figure 4-53: Default and Singlepane View Details 168
Figure 4-54: Inventory Terms & Conditions - Detail View 169
Figure 4-55: Customize Record Numbers 169
Figure 4-56: Mail Converter Configuration 170
Figure 4-57: Mail Converter Detail View 171
Figure 4-58: Mail Converter Folders 171
Figure 4-59: Mail Converter Rule Sample 172
Figure 4-60: Mail Converter Priorities 173
Figure 4-61: Mail Scan Workflow for Tickets 173

Figure 4-62: Create Workflow 174
Figure 4-63: Create Workflow Conditions 175
Figure 4-64: Workflow - Set Filter Value 175
Figure 4-65: Workflow Task Sample 178
Figure 4-66: Customer Portal Settings 179
Figure 4-67: Configuration Editor Menu 180
Figure 4-68: ModTracker Menu 182
Figure 4-69: View History in Detail View 182
Figure 4-70: ModTracker History Sample 183
Figure 4-71: Scheduler Menu 183
Figure 4-72: Webforms Setup Menu 184
Figure 4-73: Webforms - Detail View 185
Figure 4-74: Webforms - Code 186
Figure 5-1: Example I Sales Team 187
Figure 5-2: Example II Sales Team 191

List of Tables

Table 1-1: CRM Base functions 12
Table 2-1: Contact Information 25
Table 2-2: Duplicate Check During Import 28
Table 2-3: Overview event information 37
Table 2-4: Opportunity Entry Fields 48
Table 2-5: Opportunities - related lists entries 49
Table 2-6: Special default master data entry fields for quotes 52
Table 2-7: Quotes - List of default product entry fields 54
Table 2-8: Sales Orders - Special default master data entry fields 59
Table 2-9: Purchase Order - Special default master data entry fields 60
Table 2-10: Invoice - Special default master data entry fields 62
Table 2-11: Campaigns - Special default master data entry fields 65
Table 2-12: Products - Special master data entry fields 67
Table 2-13: Products - Special default master data entry fields for pricing 68
Table 2-14: Products - Products - Special default master data entry fields for stock information 69
Table 2-15: Products - Special related lists entries 70
Table 2-16: Vendors - Special default master data entry fields 73
Table 2-17: Services - Special default master data entry fields 74
Table 2-18: Services - Special default master data entry fields for service pricing information 74
Table 2-19: Service Contracts - Special default master data entry fields 76
Table 2-20: Assets - Special default master data entry fields 77
Table 2-21: Projects - Special default master data entry fields 78
Table 2-22: Project Milestone - Projects - Special default master data entry fields .. 79
Table 3-1: Outgoing Emails - Common entry fields 95
Table 3-2: Outgoing Emails - Special supporting buttons 96
Table 3-3: Incoming Mail Server Settings Fields 100
Table 3-4: Trouble Tickets - Special default entry fields 109
Table 4-1: Privilege Types 124
Table 4-2: User Login & Role - Default entry fields 131
Table 4-3: User Currency entries 132
Table 4-4: More Information - Default entry fields 133
Table 4-5: Other User Settings Information 134
Table 4-6: Sharing Permission Types 140
Table 4-7: Sharing Rules for Modules 142
Table 4-8: Layout Editor Functions 148
Table 4-9: Custom Field Definitions 149

Table 4-10: Dependency Picklist Sample	155
Table 4-11: Currency Information Fields	164
Table 4-12: Workflow - Filter Value Types	176
Table 4-13: Workflow - Formula Types	176
Table 4-14: Configuration Menu Items	180
Table 4-15: Webforms - Field Information	185

www.ingramcontent.com/pod-product-compliance
Lightning Source LLC
Chambersburg PA
CBHW081236180526
45171CB00005B/440